This volume marks the start of the Gourmet World Arc!! A new adventure begins for Toriko, Komatsu and the other Four Kings!! I'm sure that no matter the challenge, these five will prevail!! Maybe!! Well, I hope you enjoy the Gourmet World Arc!! (Meanwhile, my battle also continues!! My current weight is. . .68 kg!! Just like last time?)

–Mitsutoshi Shimabukuro, 2014

Mitsutoshi Shimabukuro made his debut in **Weekly Shonen Jump** in 1996. He is best known for **Seikimatsu Leader Den Takeshi!**, for which he won the 46th Shogakukan Manga Award for children's manga in 2001. His current series, **Toriko**, began serialization in Japan in 2008.

TORIKO

TORIKO VOL. 30
SHONEN JUMP Manga Edition

STORY AND ART BY **MITSUTOSHI SHIMABUKURO**

Translation/Christine Dashiell
Weekly Shonen Jump Lettering/Erika Terriquez
Graphic Novel Touch-Up Art & Lettering/Elena Diaz
Design/Matt Hinrichs
Weekly Shonen Jump Editor/Hope Donovan
Graphic Novel Editor/Marlene First

Printed in Canada

Published by VIZ Media, LLC
P.O. Box 77010
San Francisco, CA 94107

10 9 8 7 6 5 4 3 2 1
First printing, October 2015

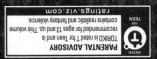

www.viz.com

TORIKO
Story and Art by
Mitsutoshi
Shimabukuro
30
ONWARD TO THE GOURMET WORLD!!

TORIKO
THE ULTIMATE GOURMET HUNTER WHO'S ON A NEVER-ENDING QUEST TO FIND AND SCARF UP THE RAREST FOODS ON EARTH! HE FIGHTS WITH A KNIFE (HIS FIST), A FORK (HIS FIST), AND SPIKED PUNCH (ALSO HIS FISTS).

WHAT'S FOR DINNER

● **KOMATSU**
TALENTED IGO HOTEL CHEF AND TORIKO'S #1 FAN.

● **COCO**
ONE OF THE FOUR KINGS, THOUGH HE IS ALSO A FORTUNE-TELLER. SPECIAL ABILITY: POISON FLOWS IN HIS VEINS.

● **SUNNY**
ONE OF THE FOUR KINGS. SENSORS IN HIS LONG HAIR ENABLE HIM TO "TASTE" THE WORLD. OBSESSED WITH ALL THAT IS BEAUTIFUL.

● **ZEBRA**
ONE OF THE FOUR KINGS. A DANGEROUS INDIVIDUAL WITH SUPERHUMAN HEARING AND VOCAL POWERS.

● **ICHIRYU**
HARDY IGO PRESIDENT AND DISCIPLE OF THE LATE GOURMET GOD ACACIA.

● **RIN**
AN IGO ANIMAL TRAINER WHO BATTLES WITH SCENT. SUNNY'S LITTLE SISTER. LOVES TORIKO.

IN THE AGE OF GOURMET, RENOWNED GOURMET HUNTER TORIKO AND TALENTED IGO HOTEL CHEF KOMATSU MEET AND BECOME PARTNERS. TOGETHER THEY TRAIN TO ENTER THE DEADLY GOURMET WORLD. TORIKO MASTERS THE SECRET ART OF "FOOD'S END" AND KOMATSU IS CELEBRATED AS ONE OF THE WORLD'S TOP 100 CHEFS.

HOWEVER, THE ANIMOSITY BETWEEN THE IGO AND RIVAL GOURMET CORP. EXPLODES INTO ALL-OUT WAR OVER GOURMET GOD ACACIA'S FULL-COURSE MEAL AND ITS MAIN COURSE, GOD. DURING THE FIGHTING, TORIKO LOSES TO STARJUN AND KOMATSU IS KIDNAPPED. IGO PRESIDENT ICHIRYU ALSO ENGAGES IN A CLIMACTIC BATTLE AGAINST GOURMET CORP. BOSS MIDORA AND MEETS A HEROIC YET TRAGIC END. THEIR CLASH ENDS WITH A RAIN OF DEADLY SPICE ANNIHILATING THE HUMAN WORLD.

THE AGE OF GOURMET IS DECLARED OVER. THE IGO IS DECIMATED, AND THE HUMAN WORLD STRUGGLES TO FIND FOOD. GOURMET CORP. ALSO TAKES HEAVY DAMAGE THANKS TO THE RISE OF A NEW POWER, NEO.

AT THE END OF THE BATTLE, TORIKO'S BODY IS RESTORED, BUT HIS STUNNING FAILURE KILLS HIS APPETITE. THAT IS, UNTIL PEOPLE RALLY TO HIS SIDE, OFFERING HIM WARM WORDS OF ENCOURAGEMENT. IT'S JUST WHAT THE DOCTOR ORDERED! HAVING SAVED KOMATSU FROM GOURMET CORP., THE PAIR HEADS TO THE GOURMET WORLD!

Contents

TORIKO

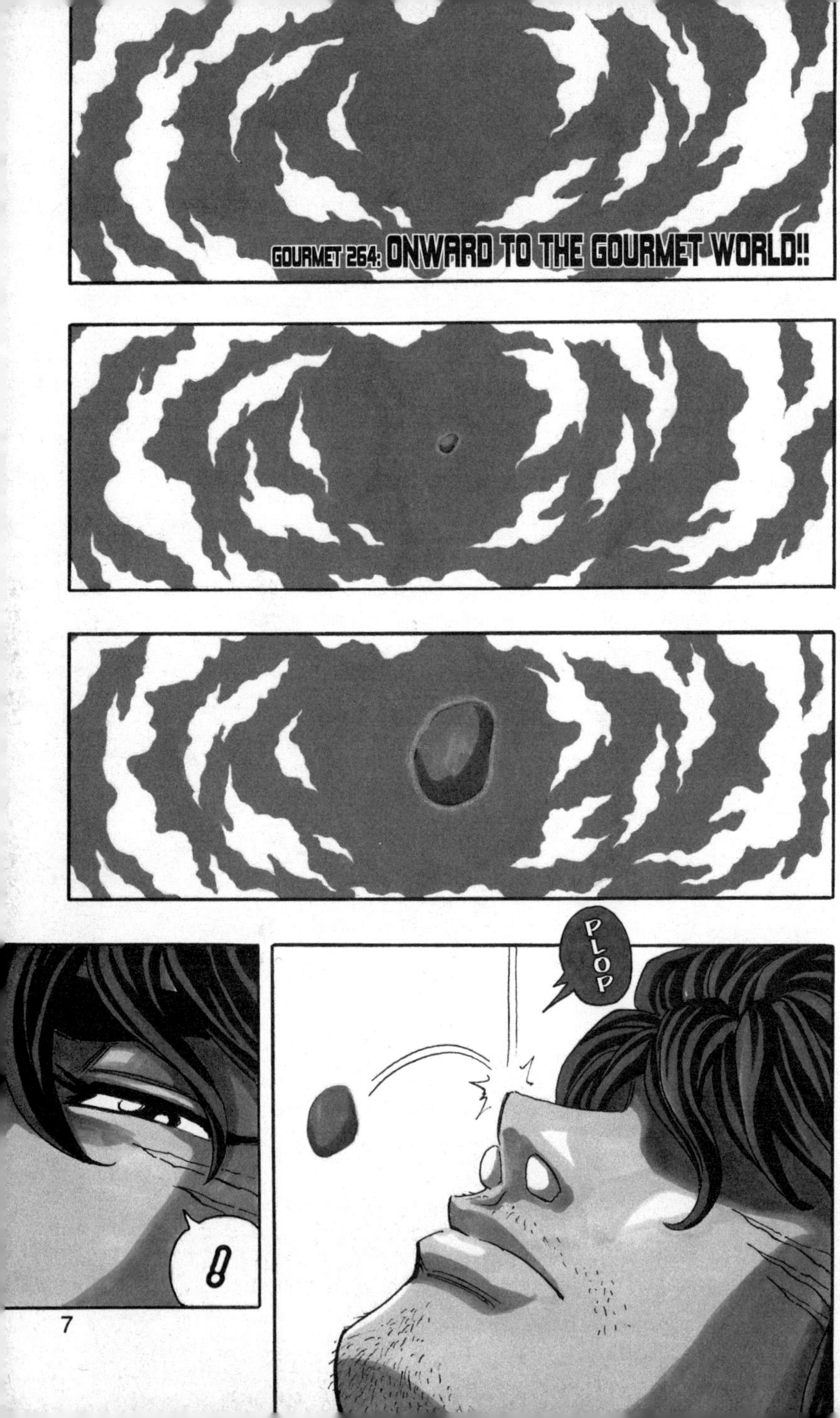
GOURMET 264: ONWARD TO THE GOURMET WORLD!!
PLOP
!

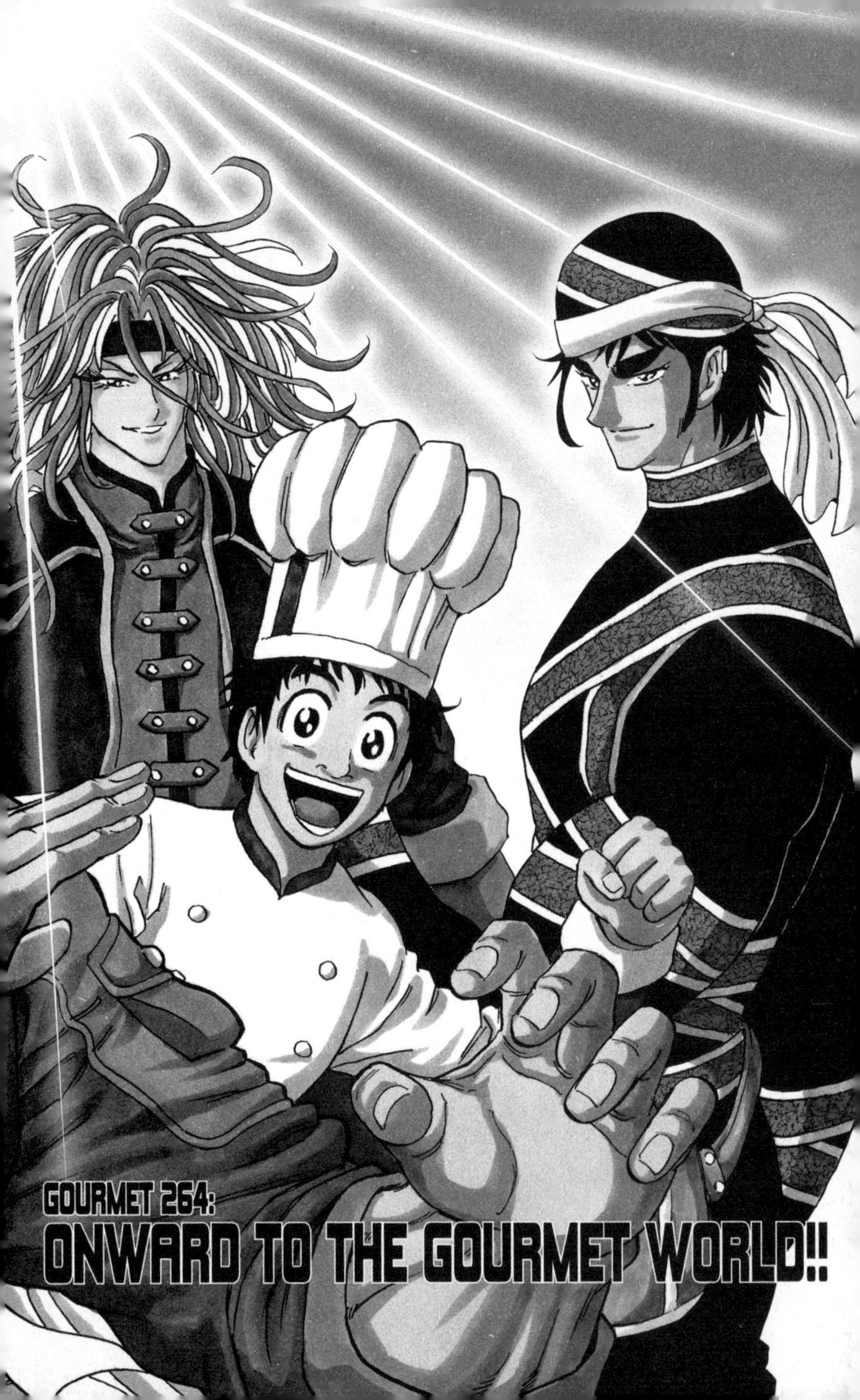
GOURMET 264:
ONWARD TO THE GOURMET WORLD!!

TORIKO

GOURMET CHECKLIST

Vol. 286

EMERALD DRAGON
(REPTILE)

CAPTURE LEVEL: 78
HABITAT: SPIRITS ARCHIPELAGO
SIZE: 50 METERS
HEIGHT: 24 METERS
WEIGHT: 350 TONS
PRICE: 5,200,000 YEN PER BOTTLE (WINE)

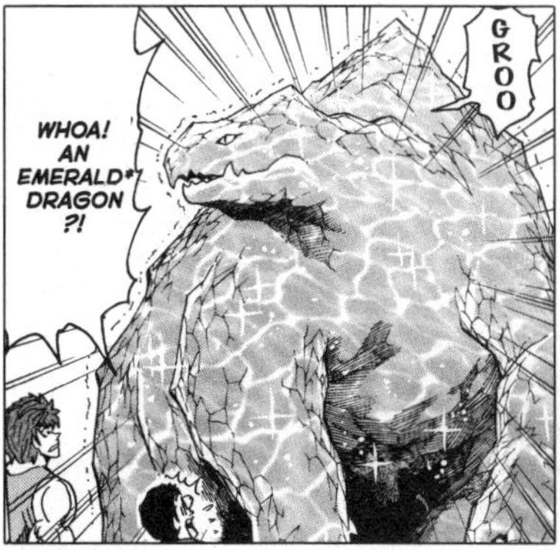

SCALE

A LEGENDARY DRAGON THAT LIVES DEEP IN THE HEART OF THE SPIRITS ARCHIPELAGO. THE EMERALD WINE THAT BUBBLES OUT OF THE SPRING ON ITS BACK GOES FOR FIVE MILLION YEN A BOTTLE. MANY TRY TO CAPTURE THE PRICEY LIQUID, BUT THE FEROCIOUS EMERALD DRAGON SENDS MOST HOPEFULS PACKING. PEOPLE WHO ARE DRUNK AND HAVE UNDUE CONFIDENCE IN THEIR ABILITIES ARE ADVISED AGAINST EVEN TRYING. YOU COULD SAY THIS DANGEROUS WINE IS TRULY FOR "STRONG" DRINKERS.

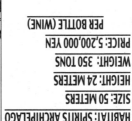

BLUB
BLUB
SPLASH
BLOOSH
CHEE
CHEE

CHEE
CHEE
CHEE
CHEE

HRNNGH!
HWAH.
HMM.
HNPH!
POP POP
THAT'S WHAT I CALL A GOOD SLEEP.
I GOT A WHOLE HOUR'S WORTH!
Haah ...
I WON'T NEED TO SLEEP FOR ANOTHER TWO WEEKS.
HM?
SNUF
SNUF
CHEE
CHEE
IS THAT ...?

IT'S A GUMDROP! ♡
TODAY'S WEATHER FORECAST:
CLEAR WITH SCATTERED ...
...GUM-DROPS!!
YAHOO! IT'S A GUMDROP DOWN-POUR!

CHOMP
CHOMP
AUHM!
CHOMP
CHOMP
CHOMP
CHOMP
GAUM.
GAUM.
GAUM.
GAUM.
CHERK
CHERK
YUM!!
THEY'RE SERIOUSLY DELICIOUS.
FOLLOWED BY A SUDDEN CHOCOLATE RAIN...
HERE IT COMES! HERE COMES THE CHOCOLATE!!
KEEP IT COMING!!
...AND SUBSEQUENT LARGE MARSHMALLOW SNOWFLAKES.
PILE UP, MARSHMALLOWS!!
DEPENDING ON THE REGION...

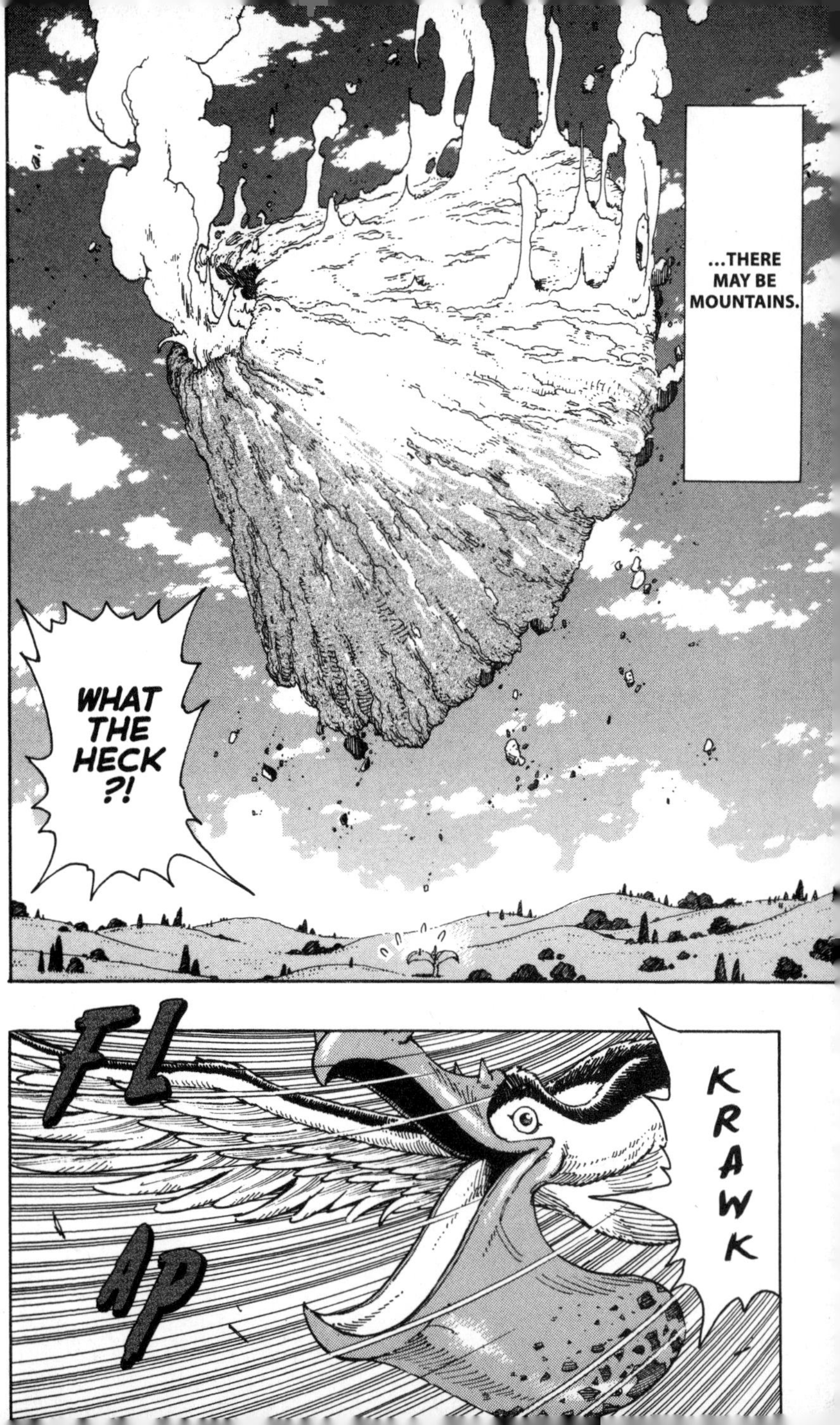
...THERE MAY BE MOUNTAINS.
WHAT THE HECK ?!
KRAWK
FL AP

WAAAAAH!
A MOUN-TAIN EATER!
HWIP
KRAWK♡
FLAP
FLAP
SEEING AS IT'S OCCUPIED...
MOUNTAIN-EATER PELICAN
(SUPER GIANT BIRD)
CAPTURE LEVEL 770
...I'LL GO AFTER THE MOUNTAIN EATER'S EGGS!
HOP
HOP
WOOOOO

HUP!
UNH!
FOUND THEM!
I'LL JUST TAKE ONE, MISS MOUNTAIN EATER.
ONE EGG ALONE WOULD MAKE ENOUGH SCRAMBLED EGGS TO FEED A HUNDRED THOUSAND PEOPLE.

FWSS—HH
...
THE LANDSEA'S PRETTY STORMY...
THIS SPOT MIGHT BECOME DANGEROUS SOON TOO...

I'VE COLLECTED ENOUGH FOOD FOR NOW.
I GUESS I'LL HEAD BACK.
Heave-ho! ♪
Heave-ho! ♪

WHOOP-
SIE
THERE!
HUP!
SWOOP
SWOOP
ROLL ROLL
WOOB
TONK
ROLL ROLL
PLOP

SIZZZZL
SIZZ
CHAK

MM-HMM. THIS PILE OUGHT TO MAKE...
...A GOOD SOUVENIR.
TAK
TAK
SSSZZZ
HEY!
I'M THINKING OF RETURNING TO THE HUMAN WORLD SOON!
WHAT DO YOU THINK ABOUT THAT...
KOMATSU?!
DUM

FINALLY, TORIKO!!
I'VE BEEN WAITING FOR THIS DAY!!
IT'S BEEN MY ONLY WISH!
BWEEH
WAF WAF
OH, OOPS!
I FORGOT TO CAPTURE A FEATHER-ROBED MUSHROOM CHILD.
WHO CARES ABOUT THE FEATHER-ROBED MUSHROOM CHILD?!
YOU CAN JUST GET A FEATHER-ROBED MUSHROOM CHILD NEXT TIME. LET'S GO HOME ALREADY, TORIKO!
YOU CAN CAPTURE A FEATHER-ROBED MUSH-ROOM CHILD ANYTIME!
AND WHAT IS A FEATHER-ROBED MUSHROOM CHILD ANYWAY?!
THE CHILD OF A MUSHROOM ?!
WHOA! YOU ATE THAT FAST!
munch munch
MAYBE YOU'RE RIGHT.
IT'S BEEN ABOUT A YEAR SINCE I CAME FOR YOU...
...AND IT'S BEEN OVER 18 MONTHS SINCE I LEFT THE HUMAN WORLD.

I'M STARTING TO GET A LITTLE WORRIED ABOUT THE HUMAN WORLD.
YUM. ♡
IT TOOK YOU LONG ENOUGH! THAT ONLY JUST CROSSED YOUR MIND?!
THIS WHOLE TIME, I'VE...
THOOM
!!
THMM-THMM
WORRYING IS YOUR JOB. RIGHT, KOMATSU?
DWAH...
WELL... YEAH...
AT LEAST 100% OF IT.
B...BUT, TORIKO...
HOW WILL WE GET ALL THIS FOOD BACK TO THE HUMAN WORLD?
I DON'T EVEN KNOW HOW WE'LL GET IT OUT THE DOOR...
I KNOW AN EASY WAY.
SWF
ZING

ICE

SL
BWOO-M
THERE.
NOW IT'LL BE EASY TO LEAVE.
COME ON, KOMATSU. TIME TO GO.

HM... NO MATTER HOW OFTEN I TRIM, MY HAIR AND BEARD GROW BACK SO QUICKLY HERE.
SHWF
SPRINKL
SPRINKL
SNIKT
FWUFF

DON'T YOU THINK YOU COULD USE A TRIM TOO?
UH... S... SURE. THANKS!
AS A CHEF, HAVING LONG HAIR IS A LITTLE--
SNIKT
IT'S SO SHORT!
That was fast!
I KNEW THAT LOOK SUITED YOU.
SINCE YOUR HAIRLINE'S SHAPED LIKE MT. FUJI.
B...BY THE WAY, TORIKO...
HOW ARE WE GOING TO *TRANSPORT* THE FOOD...
ISN'T IT OBVIOUS?
I'LL CARRY EVERYTHING ON MY SHOULDERS!
WHAAAT?!
And what's with the sparkles?
HOW ARE YOU GOING TO SHOULDER THAT?!
ON MY BACK... LIKE THIS...
NO WAY, IT'S IMPOSSIBLE! COMPLETELY IMPOSSIBLE!
IT'LL WORK.
IT WON'T!

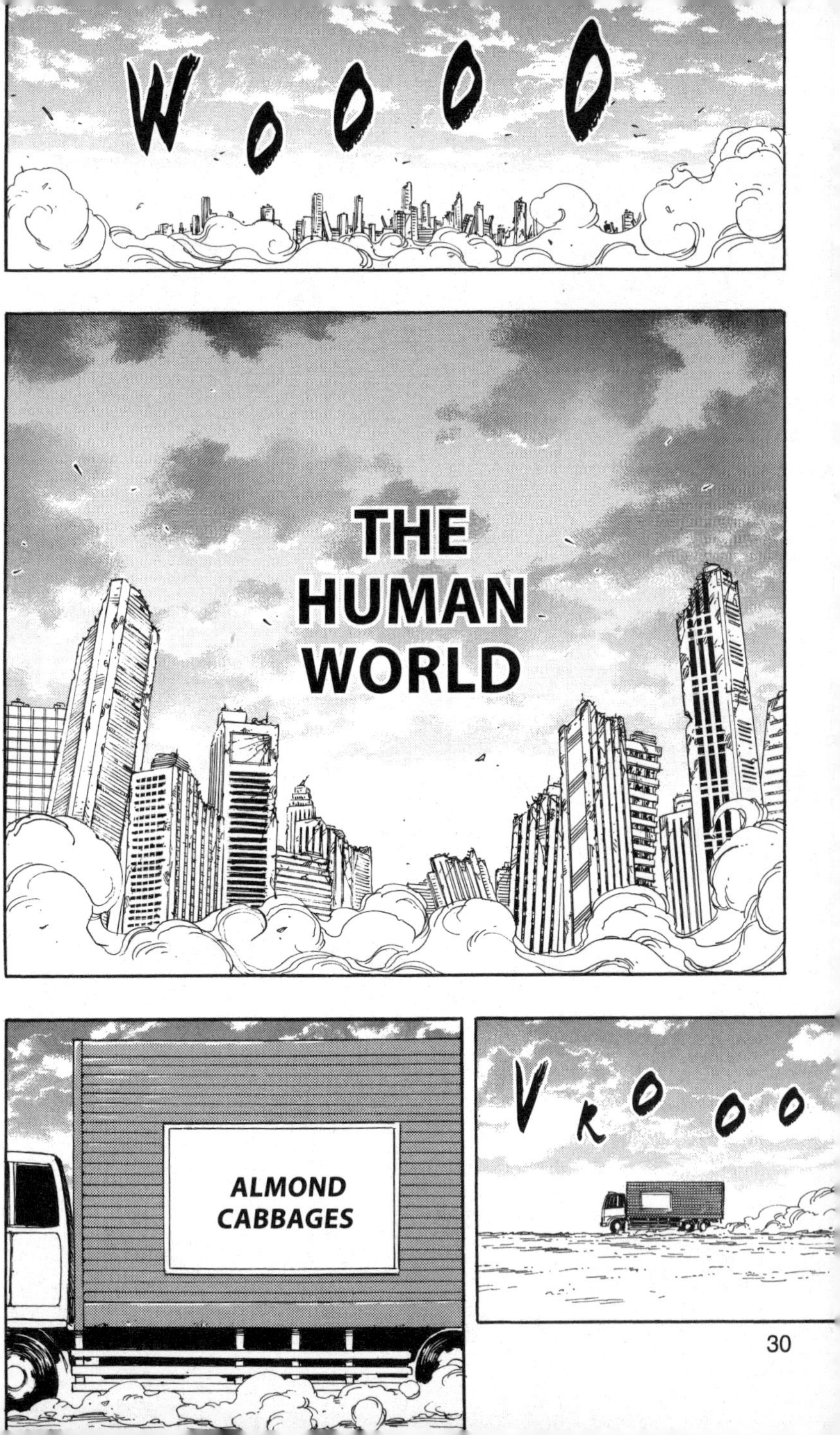
WOOOO
THE HUMAN WORLD
ALMOND CABBAGES
VROOO

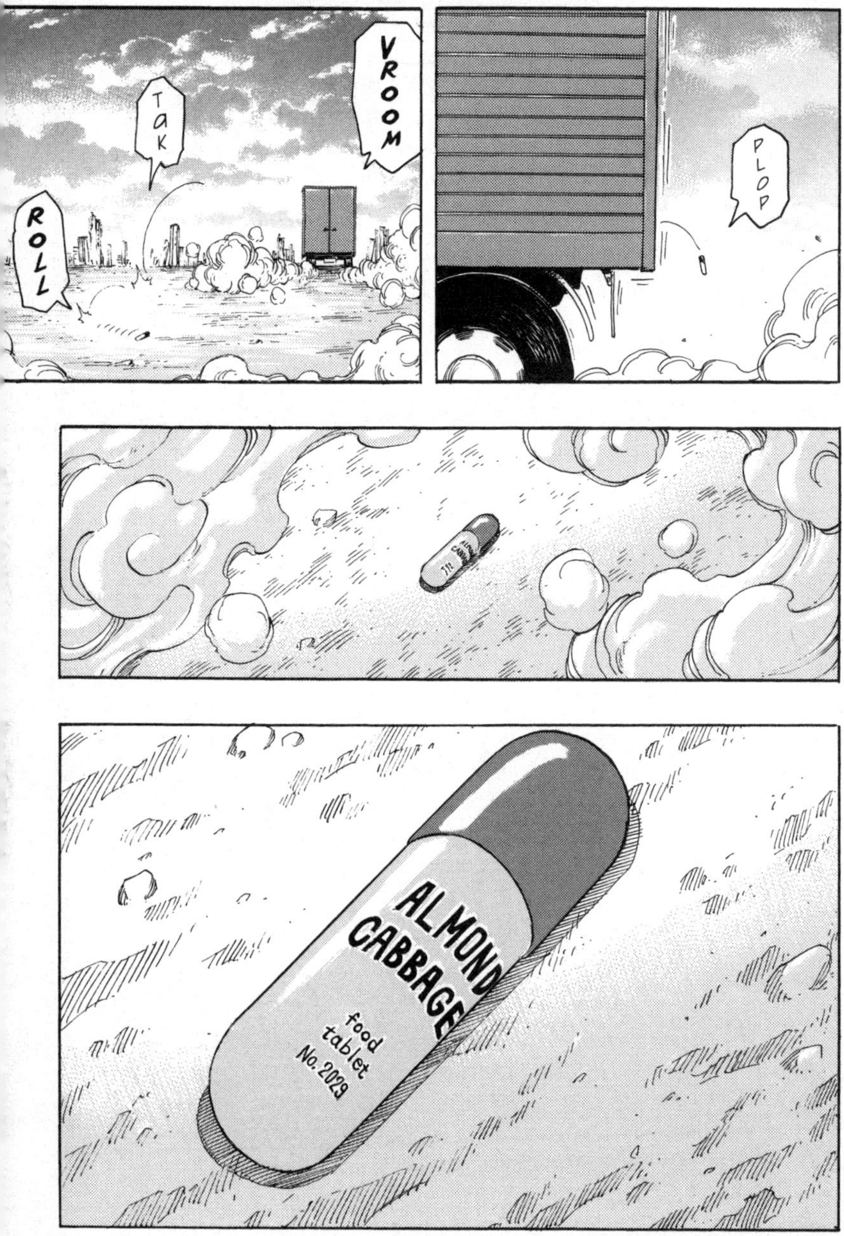
PLOP
VROOM
TAK
ROLL
ALMOND CABBAGE
food tablet
No. 2029

TORIKO

GOURMET CHECKLIST

Vol. 287

SALTED SEAWEED BUTTERFLY
(INSECT)

CAPTURE LEVEL: 1

HABITAT: SPIRITS ARCHIPELAGO

SIZE: 10 CM

HEIGHT: ---

WEIGHT: 1 G

PRICE: 1 BAG (80 G) / 450 YEN

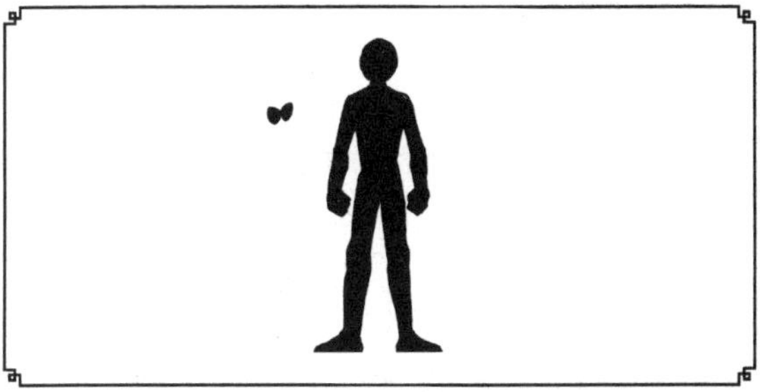

SCALE

A BUTTERFLY WITH POTATO CHIP WINGS. THEY'RE SALTED SEAWEED-FLAVORED AND ARE THE PERFECT SNACK TO ACCOMPANY A DRINK. DIFFERENT VARIETIES HAVE DIFFERENT FLAVORS, SUCH AS GARLIC, BUTTER SOY SAUCE AND OTHERS. TRYING DIFFERENT VARIETIES IS HALF THE FUN, MAKING IT A POPULAR SNACK FOR OLD AND YOUNG, BOYS AND GIRLS ALIKE!

GOURMET 265: WELCOME RAIN!!

TORIKO

GOURMET CHECKLIST

Vol. 288

KING VINEGAR
(CONDIMENT)

CAPTURE LEVEL: 57

HABITAT: SPIRITS ARCHIPELAGO

SIZE: ---

HEIGHT: ---

WEIGHT: ---

PRICE: 500 ML JUG / 350,000 YEN

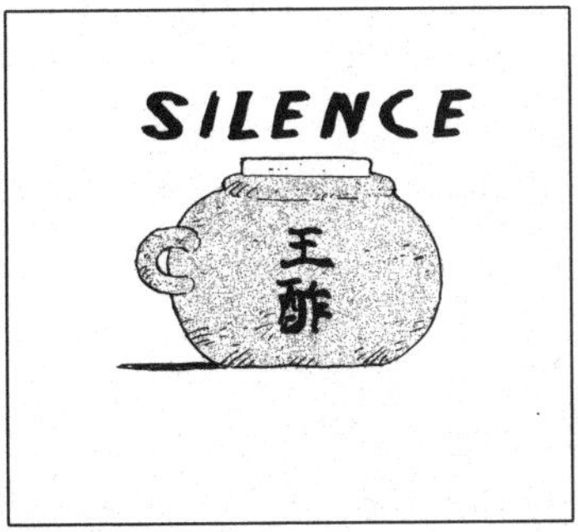

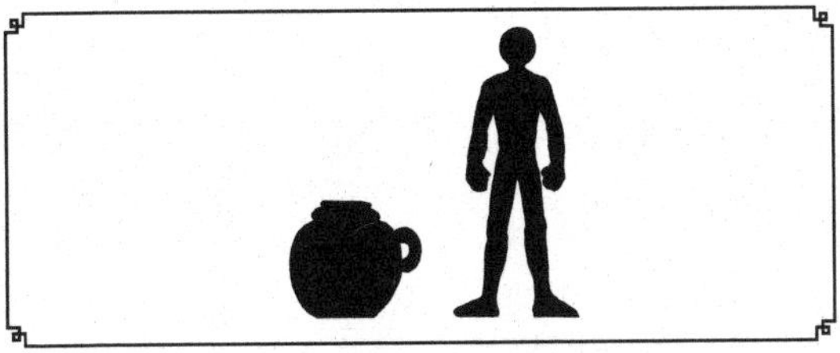

SCALE

ONE OF THE SPIRITS ARCHIPELAGO'S BEST-KNOWN FOOD PRODUCTS. WHEN IT APPEARS ON THE MARKET, IT IS CALLED THE "KING OF VINEGARS" AND IS TREATED LIKE A LUXURY FOOD. IT'LL RUN YOU 100 TIMES THE PRICE OF REGULAR VINEGAR. MULTI-STAR HIGH-CLASS SUSHI RESTAURANTS LOVE USING THE KING OF VINEGARS, AS ITS FLAVOR LEAVES LITTLE TO BE DESIRED. IT WAS AN IMPORTANT INGREDIENT IN THE FORTUNE ROLL THAT MONCHY PREPARED FOR DIVINING THE LOCATION OF CHOWLIN TEMPLE.

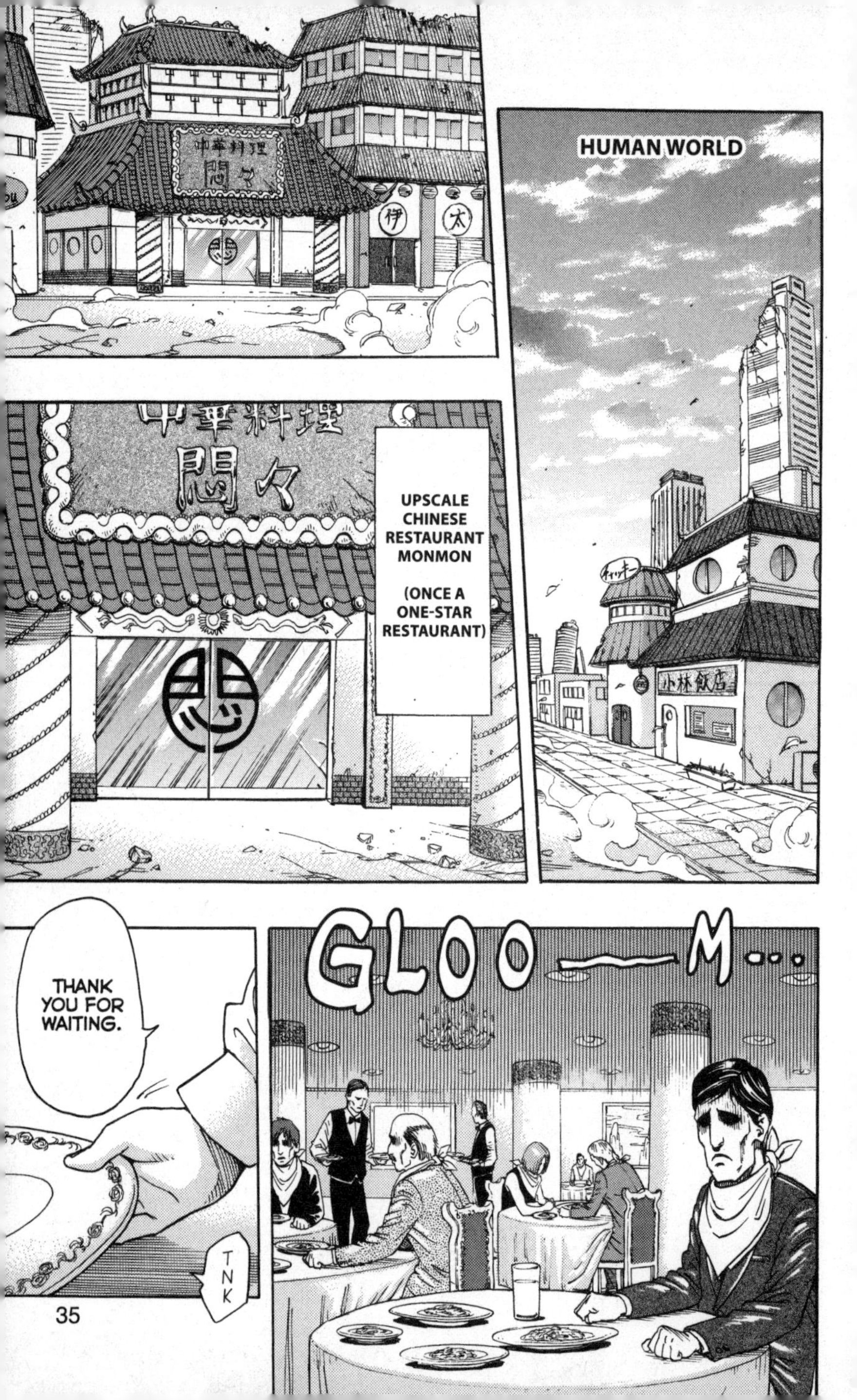
HUMAN WORLD
中華料理
悶々
UPSCALE CHINESE RESTAURANT MONMON
(ONCE A ONE-STAR RESTAURANT)
小林飯店
GLOO——M...
THANK YOU FOR WAITING.
TNK

HERE'S YOUR CRAYFISH COD, RED-HAIRED PORK...
...AND BEER LOBSTER.
I CAN'T TAKE THIS ANY-MORE !!
I'M SICK AND TIRED OF THESE BORING MEALS!!
...REAL, FRESH FOOD!!
BRING ME...
ABOUT ONE YEAR EARLIER ...

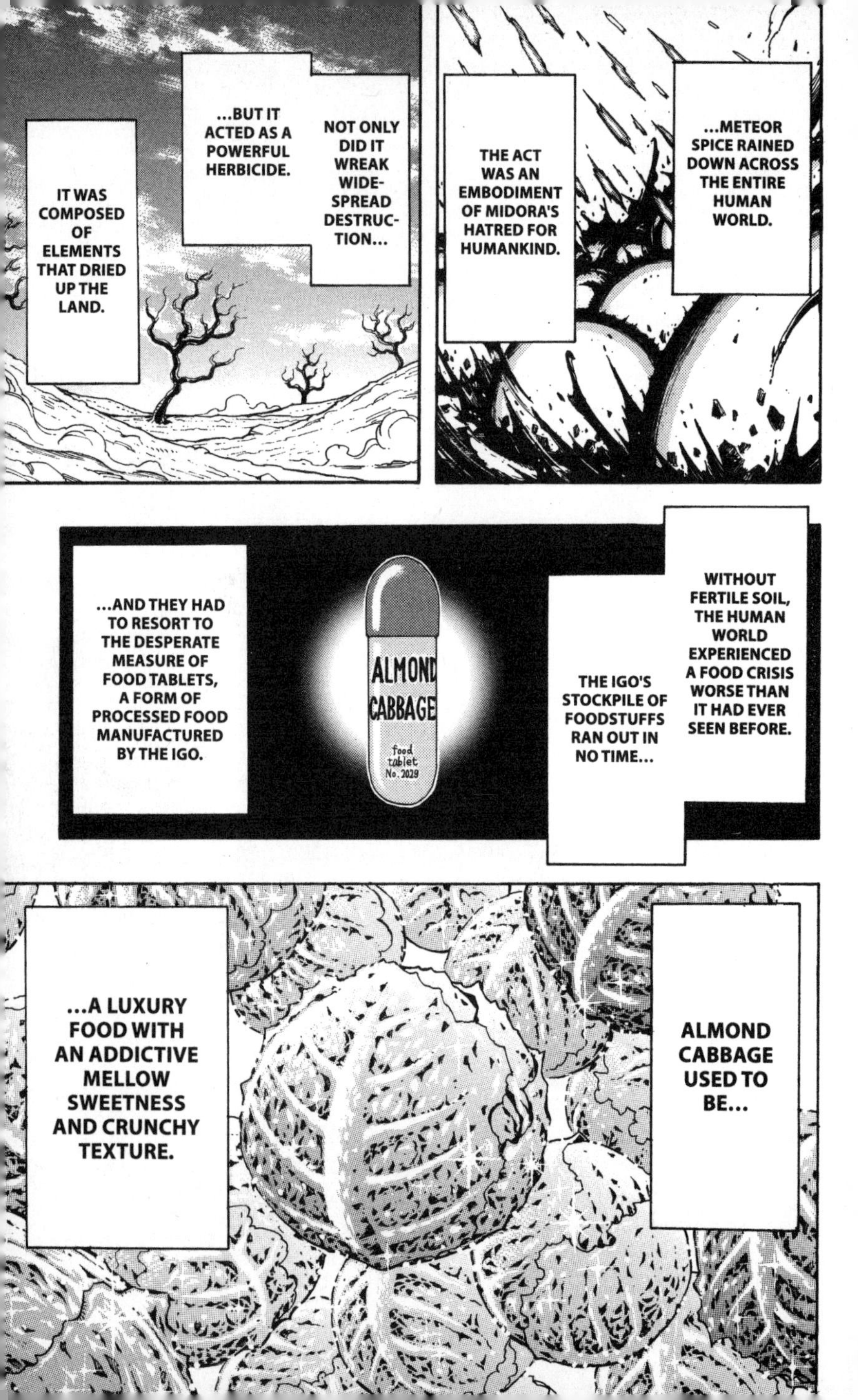
...METEOR SPICE RAINED DOWN ACROSS THE ENTIRE HUMAN WORLD.
THE ACT WAS AN EMBODIMENT OF MIDORA'S HATRED FOR HUMANKIND.
NOT ONLY DID IT WREAK WIDE-SPREAD DESTRUC-TION...
...BUT IT ACTED AS A POWERFUL HERBICIDE.
IT WAS COMPOSED OF ELEMENTS THAT DRIED UP THE LAND.
WITHOUT FERTILE SOIL, THE HUMAN WORLD EXPERIENCED A FOOD CRISIS WORSE THAN IT HAD EVER SEEN BEFORE.
THE IGO'S STOCKPILE OF FOODSTUFFS RAN OUT IN NO TIME...
ALMOND CABBAGE
food tablet No. 2029
...AND THEY HAD TO RESORT TO THE DESPERATE MEASURE OF FOOD TABLETS, A FORM OF PROCESSED FOOD MANUFACTURED BY THE IGO.
ALMOND CABBAGE USED TO BE...
...A LUXURY FOOD WITH AN ADDICTIVE MELLOW SWEETNESS AND CRUNCHY TEXTURE.

NOW, LIKE MOST FOODS, IT TOOK THE FORM OF A TABLET...
...BEING REDUCED TO ONLY ITS NUTRITIONAL VALUE...
...WHILE ITS REAL FORM DISAPPEARED FROM THE WORLD.
TMP TMP TMP
SUGI
TMP TMP
800 STORE
800 STORE
HELLO THERE.
GOOD AFTER-NOON!
GOOD AFTER-NOON, SUGURU.

WHAT A GOOD BOY, ALWAYS RUNNING ERRANDS.
IT'S A PIECE OF CAKE.
EVEN IF I BUY A BUNCH OF FOOD, IT'S NOT LIKE I HAVE MUCH TO CARRY.
HA HA HA! I GUESS SO.
HIYA, GRANNY!
WHRR
OH, SUGURU. WELCOME.
SUGI
WHAT WILL IT BE TODAY?
LET'S SEE... TEN TABLETS OF SEAWEED LETTUCE AND FIVE TABLETS OF LIGHT CARROTS, PLEASE.
Almond Cabbage
Light Carrot
Smooth Spinach
10 YEN EACH
15 YEN EACH
I'LL THROW THE CARROTS IN FOR FREE.
TNK
HOW'S YOUR MOTHER DOING?
WOW!
NO MATTER HOW OFTEN I LOOK AT THIS SYRUP DAIKON, IT ALWAYS LOOKS SO GOOD.
WELL, THE DOCTOR SAID SHE'S A LITTLE BETTER.
DAIKON USED TO BE AN EVERYDAY INGREDIENT NOT TOO LONG AGO.
BUT NOW THAT ONE'S TREATED LIKE A LUXURY ITEM JUST BECAUSE IT'S "FRESH."
RATL

I CAN'T BELIEVE WE LIVE IN A TIME WHERE WE HAVE TO KEEP DAIKON...
...BEHIND REINFORCED GLASS CASES AND HIRE GOURMET GUARDS TO PROTECT IT.
IT'S PROBABLY OVER 100 TIMES MORE EXPENSIVE THAN IT USED TO BE.
I...
I WANT TO SAVE ENOUGH MONEY...
...TO BUY FRESH FOOD SOMEDAY.
AND THEN I'LL FEED MY MOM.
THAT'S MY DREAM.
...
IF SHE COULD EAT REAL FOOD...
...I'M SURE MY MOM WOULD GET OVER HER ILLNESS!
SUGI
SU-GURU...
...

SUGURU.
HUH ?!
GRANNY, YOU CAN'T!
SHH!
THE TRUTH IS, I'LL BE CLOSING UP THIS SHOP SOON.
I DON'T HAVE MUCH REAL FOOD LEFT, BUT YOU CAN HAVE THIS, SUGURU.
SHARE IT WITH YOUR MOTHER.
B... BUT...
IT'S ALL RIGHT. I WANT TO DO THIS.
BUT IT'LL BE OUR SECRET. DON'T LET ANYBODY SEE IT.
R... REALLY ?!
W... WOW...
I FEEL LIKE I'M DREAMING.
THANK YOU, GRANNY!
THANK YOU!!
THANK YOU VERY MUCH!
TMP TMP TMP
BOO STORE

KMM
OH... OH MY GOD!
I'VE GOT REAL FOOD!
HFF
A SYRUP DAIKON!
YOU HEAR THAT, MOM?!
HFF
WAIT FOR ME, MOM.
I'M COMING HOME WITH SOMETHING REALLY AMAZING FOR YOU!
HANG IN THERE!
TRIP
AAH!
ZSHH
DON'T BLAME US.
HFF
IF YOU NEED SOME-THING TO BLAME...
HFF
...BLAME THE TIMES WE LIVE IN.
...
HUH?!

THE OLD LADY'S THE ONLY ONE WHO KNOWS THE COMBINATION TO THE STORE CASE...
HFF
HFF
THIS IS...
HFF
...THE MOMENT WE'VE BEEN WAITING FOR.
HFF
M...
MR. GUARDS...
I'LL ONLY SAY IT ONCE.
HAND OVER THAT FOOD LIKE A GOOD BOY!
HFF
HFF
PLP
PLP
...?!
Y... YOUR FINGER!!
HM... OH, RIGHT... THIS.
WHEN WE GOURMET GUARDS ARE ON DUTY, WE WEAR A LIMIT RING.
HFF
HFF
IF WE VIOLATE OUR CONTRACT IN ANY WAY WHILE WE'RE ON THE JOB, THE RING EXPLODES.
AND WE CAN'T TAKE THE RING OFF UNTIL OUR JOB'S DONE.
THIS RING IS A SYMBOL OF OUR RELIABILITY AS GOURMET GUARDS.
BUT WHAT'S THE POINT?!
OUR STOMACHS ARE SO EMPTY...
HFF
...WHAT'S IT MATTER IF WE LOSE A FINGER OR TWO?!
WE'RE STARVING!!
HFF
I TOLD YOU I'D ONLY SAY IT ONCE, DIDN'T I?!

Y...YOU CAN'T!
SHE GAVE THIS TO ME!
SHUT UP AND HAND IT OVER, YOU BRAT!
COME ON!
FORK IT OVER!
STOMP
STOMP
STOMP
N... NO!!
I'M...
MY MOM...
...GIVING THIS TO MY MOM...
SHE'S GONNA DIE ANYWAY, SO DON'T WASTE IT ON HER, YOU IDIOT!
AAH! GIVE IT BACK!!
HEH HEH HEH. AN HONEST-TO-GOODNESS PIECE OF FOOD.
HFF
IT'S LIKE WE BECAME GUARDS...
HFF
...JUST FOR THIS DAY!
I CAN'T BELIEVE OUR LUCK!
HFF
HFF
GIVE IT BACK...
I WAS GOING TO...
...GIVE IT TO MY MOM...
GIVE IT BACK...
GIVE IT BACK!!
WAAAAH!!
HYA HYAH!

ZOOOOM
THOOM
!!
WHA...
I CAN...
...SMELL IT.

WOOOO
HUH ...?
IS THAT...
...A BOWL OF FOOD?!

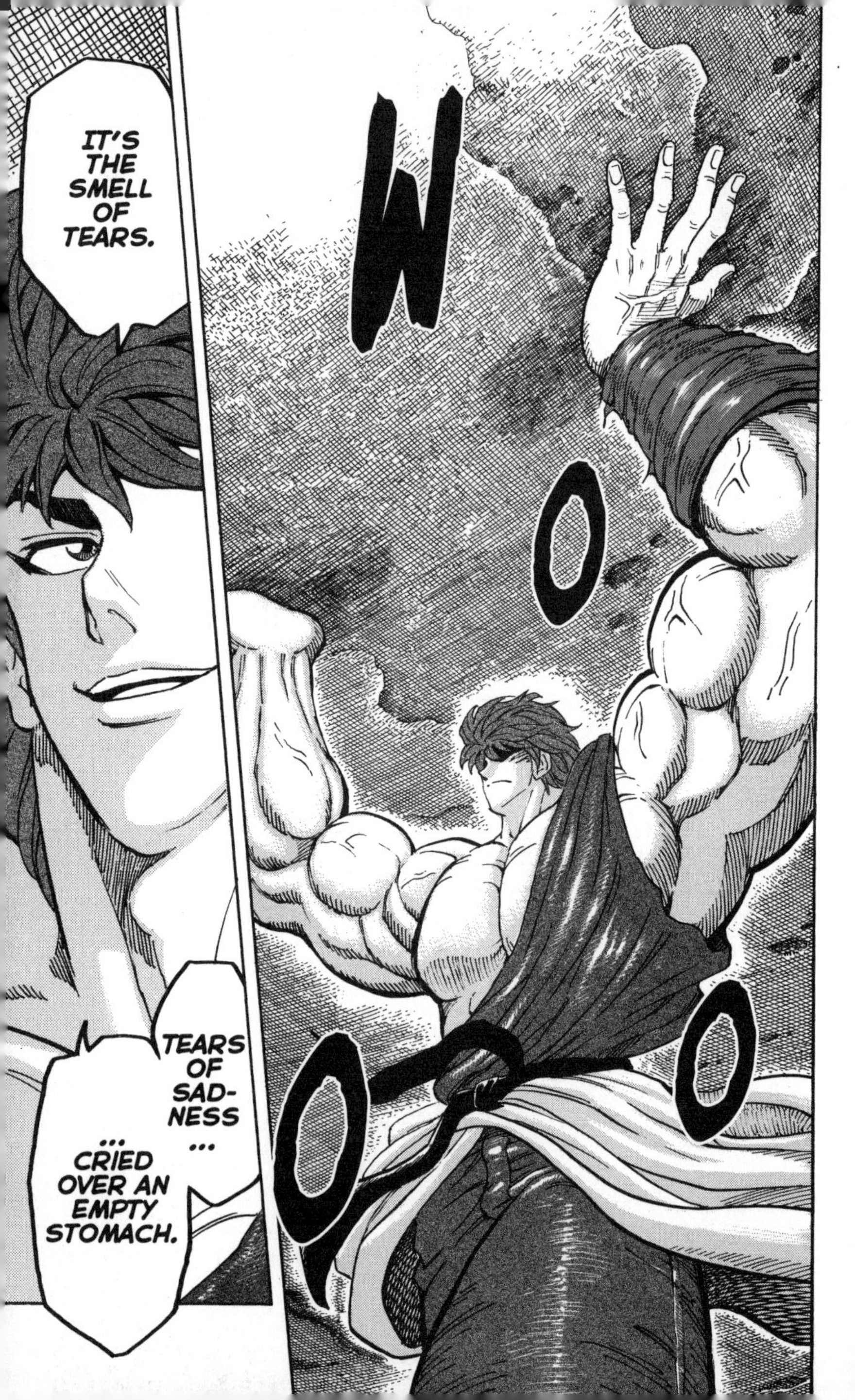
IT'S THE SMELL OF TEARS.
TEARS OF SAD-NESS ...
... CRIED OVER AN EMPTY STOMACH.
WOOOO

GRRK
GRRK
GRRK
BAM
ZOOOM
SHOOM
I SMELL IT COMING FROM OVER THERE TOO.
BAM
BAM
SHOOM
SHOOM
ENJOY YOUR SOUVENIRS ...
THIS DELICIOUS FOOD WILL RAIN DOWN...
...FROM MY TRIP TO THE GOURMET WORLD.
...AND DRENCH THE HUMAN WORLD!!

BAM BAM BAM BAM BAM
HRAAAAH!!
BAM BAM BAM BAM BAM BAM BAM BAM
BAM BAM BAM BAM BAM BAM BAM BAM BAM BAM BAM BAM
AND SO...

...A FOOD RAIN...
...COVERED THE HUMAN WORLD.
IT GENTLY WASHED AWAY PEOPLE'S SADNESS...
...AS DROPS OF HAPPI-NESS...
I KNOW...
...THAT GUY!
THAT'S HIM...
T...
TORIKO!!
GUSH
...WELLED UP FROM THEIR STOMACHS AND OVERFLOWED INTO THEIR HEARTS.

ZSSH
!
SWF
KLIK
FOOM
ZSSH
TAP
BOING
ZWISH
TAK
TAK
SSSZZZL
PLOP
PLOP
SWF
PLATE!
SSSZZZL
TUP
SSZZL

HERE.
EAT UP.
!!
BWAH
CH...
CH ...!!
CHEF KOMATSU !!
AAHH
HUH ?!
DID HE SAY TORIKO ?!
CHEF KOMA-TSU'S BACK?!
TORI-KOOO!
WAAAAH
CHEF KOMA-TSU!!
WITHOUT FOOD AND CLOTHING, PEOPLE LOSE THEIR SENSE OF REASON.
BUT YOU HAVE TO WATCH WHERE YOUR HEAD IS.
SORRY WE TOOK SO LONG.
OW... OW OW!
I THINK I BROKE SOME-THING ...

IGO HEADQUARTERS
MR. PRESIDENT!
MR. PRESIDENT!
YEAH, I KNOW.
NOM NOM
TORIKO FINALLY GOT HIS BUTT BACK HERE.
IGO PRESIDENT MANSOM
LET'S GET GOIN'...
...YOU THREE!

TORIKO

GOURMET CHECKLIST

Vol. 289

CAFÉ ANTS
(INSECT)

CAPTURE LEVEL: 1
HABITAT: MOUNTAINS
SIZE: 3 CM
HEIGHT: ---
WEIGHT: 10 G
PRICE: 50 YEN PER ANT

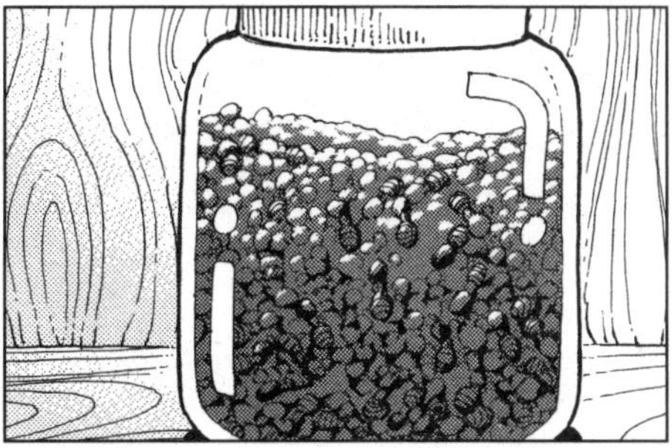

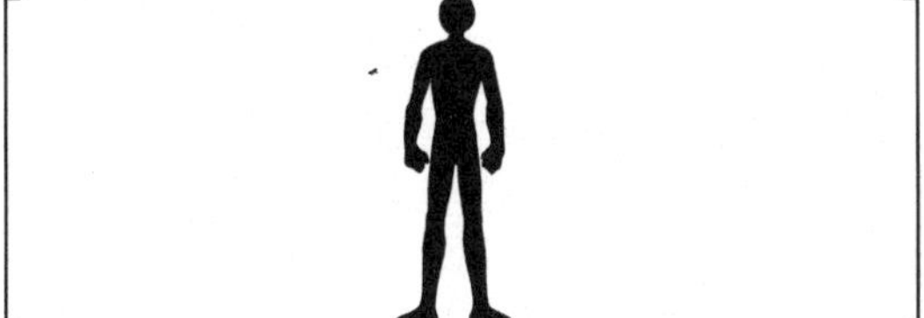

SCALE

THIS ANT'S HEAD IS MADE OF MILK, ITS THORAX IS A COFFEE BEAN AND ITS ABDOMEN IS MADE OF SYRUP. YOU CAN EAT CAFÉ ANTS RAW, BUT WHY DO THAT WHEN YOU CAN STEEP THEM IN HOT WATER FOR DELICIOUS INSTANT COFFEE? BY ADJUSTING THE AMOUNT OF HEAD-MILK AND ABDOMEN-SYRUP YOU USE, YOU CAN CREATE THE PERFECT TASTE. THE THORAX-COFFEE BEAN CAN ALSO BE GROUND UP AND BLENDED WITH OTHER COFFEES.

GOURMET 266:
FINAL TREASURE CHEST!!
SPLASH
IGO BIOTOPE 1
INSIDE THE LABORATORY
PRESIDENT'S OFFICE
YA KEPT US WAITING, TORIKO!
HOLD ON A MINUTE... DON'T TELL ME THE REASON WE WERE CALLED HERE...
...CHIEF...
IT'S NOT "CHIEF" ANYMORE.
NOW I'M...
HE IGO'S ANDSOME RESIDENT.
OH MY GOSH! GUYS!
LONG TIME NO SEE!!

HEY, KOMATSU.
I'M GLAD YOU MADE IT BACK SAFE AND SOUND.
TOOK YOU LONG ENOUGH.
LITTLE MAN...
GOURMET 266:
FINAL TREASURE CHEST!!

IF YOU'D DIED A DOG'S DEATH IN THE GOURMET WORLD...
...I WAS READY TO FOLLOW YOU TO HELL AND MANGLE YOU INTO MINCEMEAT.
I...I'M GLAD WE DIDN'T DIE THAT WAY THEN...
BEING MANGLED INTO MINCEMEAT WOULD SCARE ME TO DEATH.
HUH? MATSU, YOUR FACE LOOKS MANLIER.
LIKE IN THE NOSE.
Y...YOU THINK SO?
I KNEW IT... IT'S BECAUSE THESE PAST 18 MONTHS...
...HAVE CHANGED EVERYTHING.
SURE LOOKS THAT WAY.
YEAH.
LOOKS LIKE NOTHING MUCH'S CHANGED IN THE HUMAN WORLD.
FROM WHAT I COULD TELL.
ABOUT THAT...
THIS WAY, CHIEF!
YOU CAN SEE TORIKO NOW!
HM?

TORIKO! ♡
IGO GOURMET LABORATORY CHIEF RIN
GLOMP
THANK GOODNESS YOU'RE ALL RIGHT! ♡
I'VE BEEN SO WORRIED!
WHOA, WHOA!

BUT YOU KNOW WHAT? I ALWAYS HAD FAITH IN YOU, TORIKO!
I KNEW YOU'D COME BACK ALIVE AND WELL!!
AW... THANKS, RIN.
EVEN WHEN I WAS AT MY LOWEST POINT...
...YOU WERE LOOKING OUT FOR ME.
THE ONE...
...WHO SENT THOSE PEOPLE TO CHEER ME UP...
...WAS YOU, WASN'T IT?
THANKS, RIN.
LISTEN, TORIKO!
I CAN'T HOLD IT IN ANY LONGER, SO YOU MIND IF I JUST SAY WHAT'S BEEN ON MY MIND?
HM? AND WHAT'S THAT?
MARRY ME!
WHAT ARE YOU TALKING ABOUT?
MARRY YOU? SURE, OKAY.
I'M NOT THE KIND OF GIRL WHO'LL WAIT AROUND FOREVER...

GASP
HUH?
...
HUH?
HM?
RUB
RUB
SQUEAK
SQUEAK
GL

TORIKO, LET'S REWIND THAT.
HM?
BDMP BDMP BDMP BDMP
WILL YOU MARRY ME?
SURE, OKAY.
WHAAAAT?!
D...DO YOU REALLY MEAN IT, TORIKO?!
MAR-RIAGE?!
RIN AND TORIKO ARE GETTING MARRIED?!
WHAT'S THE MEANING OF THIS?!
UH...THE MEANING'S PRETTY OBVIOUS.
H...HOW CAN YOU DECIDE TO MARRY SOMEONE AT THE DROP OF A HAT?!
YEAH, TORIKO!! YOU'RE KOMATSU'S PARTNER ALREADY, REMEMBER?!
WHAT'S THAT GOT TO DO WITH IT?
WELL, IT DOESN'T REALLY, BUT...
DOESN'T IT?!
NOPE, IT DOESN'T.
I DON'T THINK.
WHAT ARE YOU TALKING ABOUT? EVERYBODY, CALM DOWN!!
CHIEF MANSOM, WHAT DO YOU THINK ABOUT IT?!
I'M NOT THE CHIEF... I'M THE IGO'S HANDSOME NEW PRESIDENT.
WAIT, ARE YOU TELLING ME TORIKO'S GOING TO BE MY LITTLE BROTHER?!
LOOKS LIKE IT.
GROSS ME OUT!
SO THAT MEANS YOUR PARTNER-SHIP WITH THE LITTLE MAN'S DISSOLVED.
WHY IS THAT?! EVERYBODY, CALM DOWN!!

I'VE GOT BUSINESS HERE IN BIOTOPE 1.
AND...
...THE OLD MAN'S FULL-COURSE MEAL.
...FROM WHAT I'VE SEEN OF THE HUMAN WORLD SO FAR...
...IT MEANS WE NEED ...
WE'VE SEARCHED PLENTY ALREADY.
AS YOU CAN TELL FROM THE STATE OF THE GARDEN...
...AFTER ZEBRA "SEARCHED."
HE LEFT NO STONE LEFT UNTURNED... LITERALLY.

SO YOU HAVEN'T FOUND THE *MAIN DISH* YET.
THAT'S RIGHT.
WE'RE AN EMBAR-RASSMENT TO OUR-SELVES.
GRR, IS IT EVEN REALLY IN THIS GARDEN?
THE OLD MAN'S FULL-COURSE MEAL IS SUPPOSED TO CREATE A FOOD YOU CAN EAT FOREVER, ONCE ALL THE INGREDIENTS ARE GATHERED.
ICHIRYU'S FULL-COURSE MEAL
MILLION SEED
EBOSHI TEARS
MITARASHI KELP
NOTHING BUG
?
PRINCESS STRAW SEED
DRY MEL-LON
LORD HAILSTONE
IF I REMEMBER RIGHT, ONE'S HIDDEN IN EACH BIOTOPE, IN A *TREASURE CHEST.*
I SEARCHED THE ENTIRE ISLAND USING MY ECHOLOCATION, BUT I DIDN'T FIND ANYTHING.

I COULDN'T SEE ANY ELECTRO-MAGNETIC WAVES THAT WOULD BELONG TO IT.
I ALSO SEARCHED THE ISLAND WITH MY DINING KITCHEN.
EITHER WAY, WE HAVE TO FIND IT AND FAST.
EVEN THE FOOD KOMATSU AND I BROUGHT BACK FROM THE GOURMET WORLD AS A SOUVENIR...
...IS ONLY A DROP IN THE BUCKET WITH HOW THE HUMAN WORLD IS NOW.
SHEESH...
WHY'D HE HAVE TO GO SCATTERING STUFF AROUND...
...
THIS PLACE STILL HAS A LITTLE...
...OF THE *ORIGINAL SURFACE.*
SNIFF

THE LAST THING TO PASS THROUGH HERE...
...WAS A CUCKOL-SAURUS.
A CUCKOL-SAURUS.
SO IT LEFT ITS SCENT BEHIND?
BEFORE THE CUCKOL-SAURUS...
...A ROCK DRUM WALKED HERE.
HUH?
THERE'S A TRACE OF THE ONE BEFORE IT TOO?
AND BEFORE THAT WAS AN ACCOR-DION SNAKE.
AND BEFORE THAT WAS A PIG BABOON.
AND BEFORE THAT A RAW GORGON.
AND BEFORE THAT...

THERE.

MAKE NO MISTAKE ABOUT IT.
IT WAS A WHILE BACK, BUT...
...I'M CERTAIN THE OLD MAN WALKED HERE.
S... SERIOUSLY?!
YOU CAN TELL?
NOW TO FOLLOW THE TRAIL.
THAT WAY.

...
NOT EVEN MY SIGHT CAN PICK UP ON ELECTRO-MAGNETIC WAVES OF THE PAST.
TORIKO'S ALWAYS HAD A SUPERHUMAN SENSE OF SMELL, BUT...
...I GUESS THIS PROVES THAT HIS CELLS BECAME EVEN MORE ACTIVE WHILE HE WAS IN THE GOURMET WORLD.
TORIKO ...
...DID THAT IN THE GOURMET WORLD TOO.
!
HE WOULD USE TRACES OF MY SMELL...
...AS A COMPASS TO FIND ME.
EVERY DAY, IN AND OUT.
TORIKO TOLD ME THAT HE COULD SENSE MY PRESENCE ...
...LIKE IT WAS A TANGIBLE THING.

...
IS THAT SO?
IT'S NOT JUST TORIKO.
KOMATSU TOO...
...HAS SURPASSED OUR EXPECTATIONS OF HIM.
EVERY INCH OF THE GOURMET WORLD...
...IS WHAT THE HUMAN WORLD WOULD CALL A "DANGER ZONE."
BUT EVERY ONCE IN A WHILE, RELATIVELY SAFE SPOTS POP UP.
I NAMED THEM "GOURMET WORLD REST ROOMS."
THEY'RE TEMPORARY SAFE SPOTS THAT ARISE FROM UNIQUE CLIMATES AND SPECIAL ECOSYSTEMS.
THE HUMAN WORLD HAS TREES AND ROCKS LIKE THE SYCNOMORE TREES THAT MAKE UP THE DISAPPEARING FOREST AND VANISHING JAPANESE CUISINE.
SIMILARLY, THE GOURMET WORLD HAS COWARDLY AIR THAT GIVES RISE TO INVISIBLE SPACES.

THE REST ROOMS ARE BLIND SPOTS TO MONSTERS.
THEY'RE ONLY TEMPORARY, BUT THEY'RE PEACEFUL AND QUIET.
HUH.
I'M SURPRISED THERE ARE PLACES LIKE THAT IN THE GOURMET WORLD.
IT'S LIKE...
...THEY'RE IN ANOTHER TIME AND SPACE.
AN ISOLATED SPACE.
SNIFF
IN THE GOURMET WORLD, SUCH PLACES...
...GET SQUEEZED OUT BY THE SURROUNDING ENVIRONMENT AFTER ENOUGH TIME'S PASSED.
BUT WHAT IF THERE WAS A PLACE LIKE THAT IN THE HUMAN WORLD?
THE OLD MAN ALWAYS DID ENJOY A GOOD PRANK.
OR IS THIS JUST CHANCE?

WHY IS THAT THE ONLY PLACE...
...STILL IN PRISTINE CONDITION?
EVEN THOUGH ZEBRA TRASHED THE REST OF THE ISLAND.
HM.
NOW THAT YOU MEN-TION IT...
...YOU'VE GOT A POINT.
OUT OF COCO'S FIELD OF VISION.
OUT OF ZEBRA'S EAR-SHOT.
OUT OF SUNNY'S HAIR'S REACH.
BUT MY NOSE...
...CAN SMELL IT CLEARLY.
EVERY ROOM'S GOT TO HAVE A DOOR.
YOU CAN'T GET IN UNTIL YOU FIND IT.
MOOSH
BINGO.

SHWIP
HUH?!
WHAT THE?!
HE'S GONE!
GUYS, I FOUND IT!
COME ON! OUR TREASURE HUNT'S OVER!
HE DID IT!
LET'S GO, EVERY-ONE!
...
OH WOW!!
WE REALLY CAN GET IN!
MWSH
SOMEHOW... THE AIR FEELS REALLY THICK...
OOOH! I CAN'T BELIEVE BIOTOPE 1...
MWSH
...HAD A PLACE LIKE THIS IN IT!

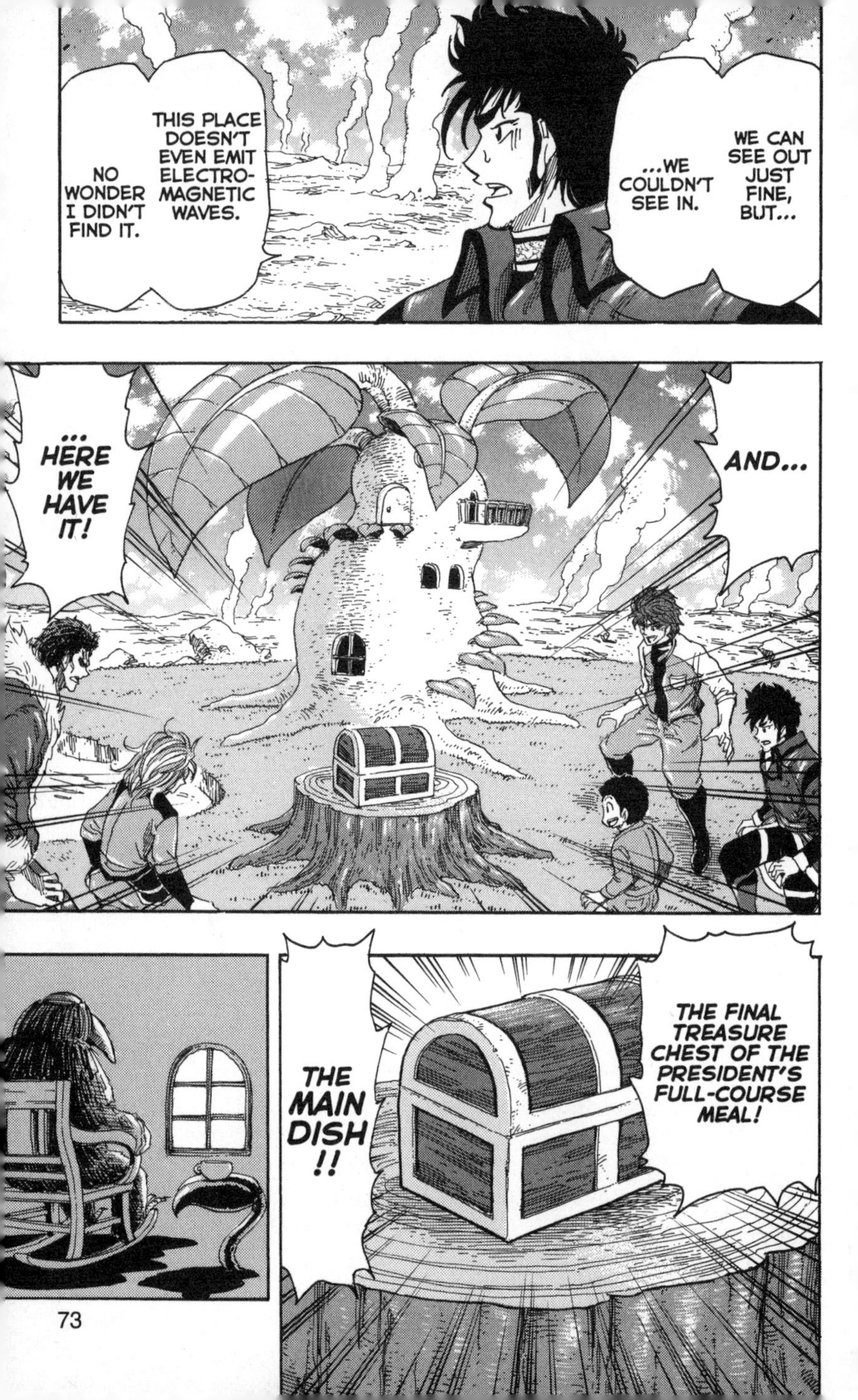
WE CAN SEE OUT JUST FINE, BUT...
...WE COULDN'T SEE IN.
THIS PLACE DOESN'T EVEN EMIT ELECTRO-MAGNETIC WAVES.
NO WONDER I DIDN'T FIND IT.
AND...
...HERE WE HAVE IT!
THE FINAL TREASURE CHEST OF THE PRESIDENT'S FULL-COURSE MEAL!
THE MAIN DISH!!

TORIKO

GOURMET CHECKLIST

Vol. 290

SALMON ROE GRAPES

(FRUIT)

CAPTURE LEVEL: 2

HABITAT: REVIVED BY TEPPEI

SIZE: 18 CM (ONE BUNCH)

HEIGHT: ---

WEIGHT: 350 G (ONE BUNCH)

PRICE: 8,000 YEN (ONE BUNCH)

THESE ARE SALMON ROE GRAPES.*
THEY DISAP-PEARED FROM THE WILD FORTY YEARS AGO, BUT JUST THE OTHER DAY I REVIVED THEM.

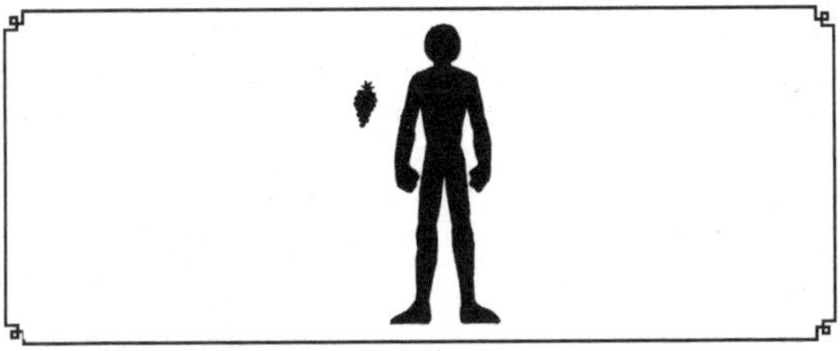

SCALE

A DECIDUOUS SHRUB IN THE GRAPE FAMILY. THE FRUIT HAS THE TEXTURE AND BEAUTIFUL VIVID TRANSLUCENCY OF COD ROE. IT SMELLS AND TASTES FRESH, NOT FISHY. RAW, SALMON ROE GRAPES GO WELL WITH SOY SAUCE. IF PICKLED IN IT, PICKLED COD ROE GRAPES ARE A NICE BAR SNACK. THESE GRAPES VANISHED FROM THE WILD FORTY YEARS AGO, BUT WERE RECENTLY REVIVED BY TEPPEI.

GOURMET 267: BIRTH CRY OF HOPE!!

OOOOM
GOURMET 267: BIRTH CRY OF HOPE!!
...
TORIKO! LET'S GET GOING ALREADY!
RIGHT.

BIOTOPE 1
CULTIVATE COURT 17
17 COURT
WOW! IT'S EVERY-ONE!
LONG TIME NO SEE!
CHEF KOMATSU.
GLAD TO SEE YOU'RE ALL RIGHT.
SAME TO YOU.
I'M SO HAPPY TO SEE YOU ALL AGAIN.
SNFL
KOMA-TSU.
CHIRU!
THE OTHERS ...

THE OTHER CHEFS ...
...WERE TAKEN AWAY.
...
BY THE TIME I ARRIVED ...
...GOURMET CORP. HEAD-QUARTERS HAD BEEN DESTROYED.
IT WAS COMPLETELY EMPTY...NOT A CHEF IN SIGHT.
THERE WAS PRACTICALLY NOBODY LEFT BUT KOMATSU.
THE ONLY ONES WAITING FOR ME WERE KOMATSU ...
...AND ONE OTHER PERSON.
E... EVERY-ONE...
...WAS TAKEN SOME-WHERE ELSE.
BUT...
I KNOW THEY'RE ALIVE!
THEY HAVE TO BE!
IN-DEED ?
IF THEY'RE ALIVE, THEN A CHANCE REMAINS TO RESCUE THEM.
IF WE ARE TO RESTORE THE HUMAN WORLD TO ITS PREVIOUS STANDARDS OF DINING...
...WE SHALL NEED THE HELP OF MANY CHEFS.

AND MOST IMPORTANTLY...
...OF A GOOD NUMBER OF INGREDIENTS.
THAT'S WHY WE'VE GATHERED TODAY.
IT WOULD BE A MILLIMETER MORE ACCURATE TO SAY WE WERE SUMMONED.
BY THE VOICES OF THESE FOODS.
THIS IS...
...ICHIRYU'S FULL-COURSE MEAL.
WHAT MAIN DISH IS RESIDING IN THE GOURMET CASE?
YOU ALREADY KNOW, DON'T YOU?
LIVE-BEARER.
LIVE-BEARER, YOU CAN HEAR THE VOICES TOO?
NOPE, I HAVEN'T HEARD A THING.
YOU HAVEN'T ?!
BUT I KNOW WHAT'S INSIDE...
...THANKS TO SOME DATA I INGESTED.
IT'S AS EASY AS THAT.
OKAY... I'M OPENING IT.
CLIK
PSSHT

IT'S...
...AN EGG ...?!
THE EGG OF THE RARE...
... BILLION BIRD!
B...
BIL-LION BIRD ?!
I'VE HEARD OF IT.
IT'S A BIRD THAT LIVED IN THE GOURMET WORLD IN ANCIENT TIMES.
THE BILLION BIRD...

ITS MEAT IS HIGH IN PROTEIN AND AGREEABLY JUICY.
ITS WINGS CONTAIN A RICH SUPPLY OF VITAMINS AND MINERALS.
AND ITS LEGS AND TALONS ARE PACKED WITH NUTRITION. THEY CAN EVEN BE USED AS A PRESERVATIVE.
MOST STRIKING OF ALL IS ITS FERTILITY.
ONCE BORN, NO MATTER WHAT ITS ENVIRONMENT ...
...IT CAN LAY FERTILIZED EGGS ALMOST INDEFINITELY.
INDEFINI-TELY ...?!
IS THAT EVEN POSSIBLE ...?
WHAT'S MORE, THE BILLION BIRD'S LIFE SPAN IS SAID TO LAST SEVERAL THOUSANDS, IF NOT SEVERAL HUNDREDS OF MILLIONS OF YEARS.
THE BIRD THAT YOU CAN EAT FOR A BILLION YEARS. LONG AGO, IT WAS EVEN CALLED THE KING OF LIVESTOCK.
I CAN'T BELIEVE ICHIRYU'S FULL COURSE...
...IN-CLUDED THAT BIRD.
WE WERE CALLED...
...FOR ONE REASON.
YES.

WITH THIS BIRD...
...WE CAN FILL THE BELLY OF EVERY PERSON ALIVE!
LET'S INCUBATE THE EGG RIGHT AWAY!
GRAB
DON'T WORRY, HUMAN WORLD, YOU'LL HAVE REAL FOOD SOON!
CHEF KOMA-TSU...
WHAT ON EARTH ARE YOU DOING...?
WHAT ELSE ?!
I'M KEEPING IT WARM! SO THAT THE EGG WILL HATCH!
COME ON, EVERYONE! WE'LL TAKE TURNS KEEPING IT WARM!!
WE DON'T HAVE A MOMENT...
...TO LOSE!
MATSU! WHAT KIND OF IDIOT ARE YOU?!
THAT'S NOT HOW IT WORKS!
SMACK
HUH?
IT GOES LIKE THIS!
YOU'VE GOT TO RUB IT!
RUB RUB RUB RUB
I SEE...
YOU'RE BOTH IDIOTS...

WE JUST BUST IT OPEN AND FORCE IT TO HATCH.
OUTTA THE WAY.
ARE YOU CRAZY, YOU IDIOT?! STOP IT!!
I'M... SORRY ABOUT ALL THIS...
A BILLION BIRD EGG CAN ONLY INCUBATE AND HATCH UNDER CERTAIN CONDITIONS.
...IS CONTAINED ...
...IN THE OLD MAN'S FULL-COURSE MEAL.
EVERYTHING WE NEED TO CREATE THOSE CONDITIONS ...
O... OKAY...
UH... LIVE-BEARER, AM I RIGHT?
YEP.

FIRST
...
...IS THE OLD MAN'S APPETIZER, THE *MILLION TREE.*
THIS SEED.
THE BILLION BIRD'S EGG WILL ONLY HATCH IN A NEST BUILT IN A *MILLION TREE.*
PLOP
THE OLD MAN'S SOUP IS *EBOSHI TEARS.*
PLOP
PLOP
SHOOM
THE LIQUID WRUNG OUT OF IT FERTILIZES THE MILLION SEED...
...MAKING IT SPRING UP INSTANTLY.
ZWOOOP
OOH!
FWOOM
NEXT COMES THE NEST.
THE FULL-COURSE'S SALAD IS *PRINCESS STRAW SEED.*
THE EGG WON'T HATCH UNLESS THE NEST IS MADE FROM THIS STRAW.
PLMP

HIS FULL-COURSE DRINK IS LORD HAILSTONE.
FLK
FLK
IT'S THE NUTRIENT FOR THE STRAW.
...AND PUT IT AT THE TOP OF THE MILLION TREE.
NOW THE NEST IS COM-PLETE!
THE PRINCESS STRAW GROWS...
FS SHH
...AND WE TAKE IT...
NEXT WE WAIT...
...FOR THE EGG TO HATCH.
HOW LONG UNTIL IT HATCHES?
I CAN ALREADY SEE ITS ELECTRO-MAGNETIC WAVES.
I HEAR A HEART-BEAT.
IT'LL BE A COUPLE DAYS.
RIGHT, WE'LL PREPARE OUR RESTAURANTS FOR THAT DAY.
OUR RESTAURANTS HAVE BEEN CLOSED DOWN ALL THIS TIME WE HAVEN'T HAD INGREDIENTS.
GOOD IDEA!
JUST WAIT FOR AN ANNOUNCEMENT OF ITS BIRTH!

17 COURT
HEY, TORIKO.
HMM?
IF THE BILLION BIRD IS SO INCREDIBLE...
...HOW COME NOBODY HAS PAID ATTENTION TO IT BEFORE?
WHY ELSE?
BECAUSE IT *TASTES TERRIBLE.*
THE BILLION BIRD...
...CAN'T FLY AND HAS LOTS OF NATURAL ENEMIES.
SO AS A MEANS OF DEFENSE, IT LAYS AN EGG EVERY TIME IT'S ATTACKED.
AND IT CAN DO THAT NONSTOP.

BUT WHAT'S THE POINT OF HAVING SOMETHING YOU CAN EAT FOREVER...
...IF IT DOESN'T TASTE GOOD?
EVENTUALLY, NO MORE CREATURES ATE THE BILLION BIRD.
BECAUSE IT WAS NEVER ATTACKED, IT STOPPED LAYING EGGS.
EVENTUALLY, PEOPLE BELIEVED IT HAD GONE EXTINCT.
A BIRD THAT COULD LIVE FOR THOUSANDS OF YEARS WENT EXTINCT...
...ALL BECAUSE...
...NOBODY WANTED TO EAT IT.
THAT'S THE AGE OF GOURMET FOR YOU.
CAN'T DO ANYTHING ABOUT THAT.
...
SETSUNO ONCE SAID...
...THAT CHEFS DON'T CHOOSE THEIR INGREDIENTS.
THE INGREDI-ENTS...
...CHOOSE THEIR CUSTOMERS AND CHEFS.
THE BILLION BIRD...
...MUST HAVE CHOSEN US NOW.

WE...
...WANT YOU, BILLION BIRD!
WE CAN'T WAIT FOR YOU...
...TO BE BORN ALIVE AND HEALTHY.
WE CAN'T WAIT.
KRAK
MYO
MYO
AH!

MYO
MYO
AAAH!
IT HATCHED, EVERY-ONE!!
IT HATCHED!
OH, FOR REAL?!
HOW'S IT LOOK?!
WHOA, WHAT AN UGLY LITTLE BILLION BIRD!
GROSS!
IT'S ADORABLE!
TRMBL TRMBL
MYO MYO
IT'S STILL JUST A CHICK.
NOW TO TURN IT INTO AN ADULT!
THE FISH COURSE OF THE OLD MAN'S FULL-COURSE MEAL IS MITARASHI KELP.
IT'S THE FOOD YOU GIVE THEM WHEN THEY'RE CHICKS. HERE, EAT UP.
MYO MYO
CHEW CHEW
BOOMF
WHOA!

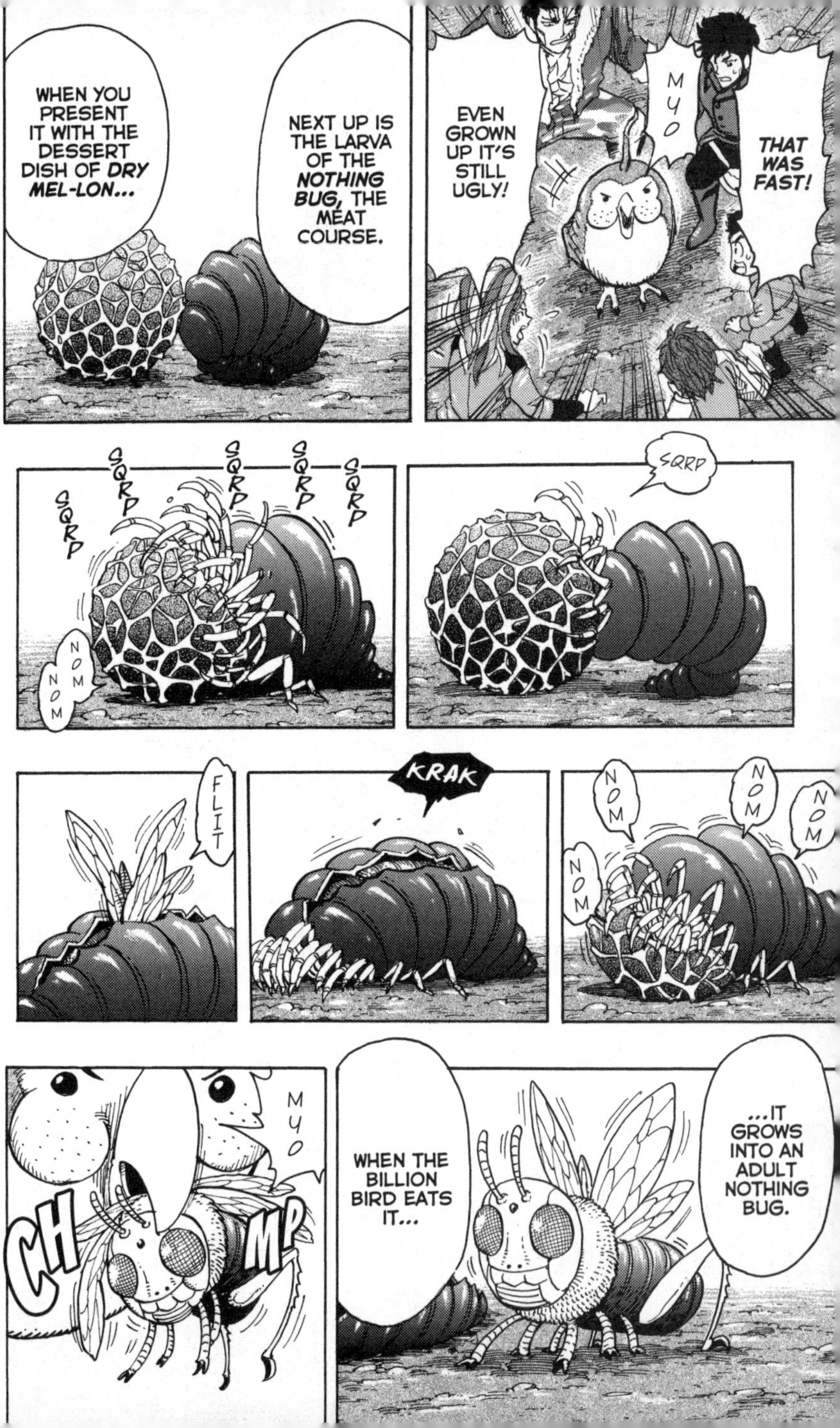
THAT WAS FAST!
MYO
EVEN GROWN UP IT'S STILL UGLY!
NEXT UP IS THE LARVA OF THE NOTHING BUG, THE MEAT COURSE.
WHEN YOU PRESENT IT WITH THE DESSERT DISH OF DRY MEL-LON...
SQRP
SQRP SQRP SQRP SQRP
NOM NOM
NOM NOM NOM NOM
KRAK
FLIT
...IT GROWS INTO AN ADULT NOTHING BUG.
WHEN THE BILLION BIRD EATS IT...
MYO
CHMP

KRCH
KRCH
VOOP
ZWOOOP
WE DID IT! NOW THE BILLION BIRD...
...IS READY TO START LAYING EGGS INDEFINITELY!
ZING
WHAT THE BILLION BIRD NEEDS NOW...
...IS A GOOD SCARE...
RAAAAH!!
GYAK
MYO!!
TWIK
TWIK
OOM

POOM POOM POOM
POOM POOM POOM
POOM POOM
POOM POOM
POOM POOM
MYOOOO
OH MY GOSH!!
W... WE DID IT!
THE BILLION BIRD LAID EGGS!
AND IF THE PARENT BIRD IS FOUNDATION STOCK, THEN THE EGGS...
...HATCH RIGHT AWAY!
KRAK

THIS IS THE OLD MAN'S FULL-COURSE MEAL!
MYO
MYO
MYO
MYO
THE NEVER-ENDING FOOD--BILLION BIRD!
NOW THE HUMAN WORLD...
LEAVE THE COOKING TO ME!
I PROMISE THAT WE CHEFS OF THE HUMAN WORLD...
...IS SAVED!
EVEN THOUGH THE BIRD'S HIDEOUS!
...WILL COOK IT INTO SOMETHING DELICIOUS!
IT DOESN'T MATTER HOW IT LOOKS. JUST HOW IT TASTES.
THAT'S THE PROBLEM.

TORIKO

GOURMET CHECKLIST

Vol. 291

MOCHI ROCK
(MINERAL)

CAPTURE LEVEL: 3

HABITAT: REVIVED BY TEPPEI

SIZE: 15 CM

HEIGHT: ---

WEIGHT: 450 G

PRICE: 3,900 YEN PER ROCK

MOCHI ROCKS* ARE CANDY-LIKE STONES FOUND IN STRATUM SEVERAL THOUSAND YEARS OLD.
I'VE ALMOST GOT THEM REVIVED.
AWESOME! THE MARKET'S GONNA EAT THEM UP!

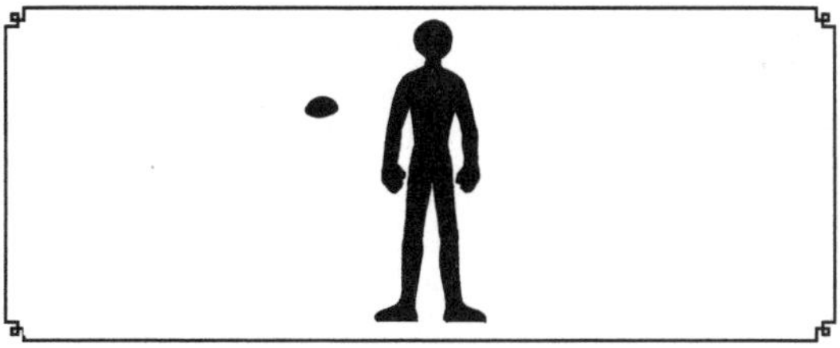

SCALE

A MOCHI-LIKE MINERAL DISCOVERED IN STRATUM SEVERAL THOUSAND YEARS OLD. FOR SOMETHING CLASSIFIED AS AN INORGANIC CRYSTAL, MOCHI ROCK IS REMARKABLY SOFT. IT TASTES DELICIOUS AND IS SURMISED TO BE AN ANCIENT CREATURE PRESERVED IN STRATUM FROM THE TIME IT LIVED. THERE ARE MANY DIFFERENT VARIETIES OF IT THAT OFFER FLAVORS SUCH AS SWEET RED BEAN, SOY SAUCE, SWEET SOYBEAN AND ROASTED SOY FLOUR.

MY—O!
SO THIS IS THE OLD MAN'S FULL-COURSE MEAL!
THE BILLION BIRD!
GOURMET 268: MIRACLE EGG!!
AMAZING! THEY JUST KEEP MULTIPLYING!
LEAVE THE COOKING TO US!
I PROMISE THAT WE CHEFS OF THE HUMAN WORLD...
...WILL COOK IT INTO SOMETHING DELICIOUS!
GOOD! LET'S DELIVER BILLION BIRD...
...ACROSS THE GLOBE RIGHT AWAY!

GOURMET 268: MIRACLE EGG!!
GAB
GAB
DAMARASU CURRY
DAMARASU CURRY
FLAGSHIP RESTAURANT
BLUB
BLUB
INCREDIBLE...! WHEN BILLION BIRD FEET ARE DRIED AND CHOPPED, THEY CAN BE USED AS A SUBSTITUTE FOR RICE.
TALONS CAN BE USED AS-IS FOR SPICE...
...AND THE MEAT, OF COURSE, IS THE CENTER-PIECE.

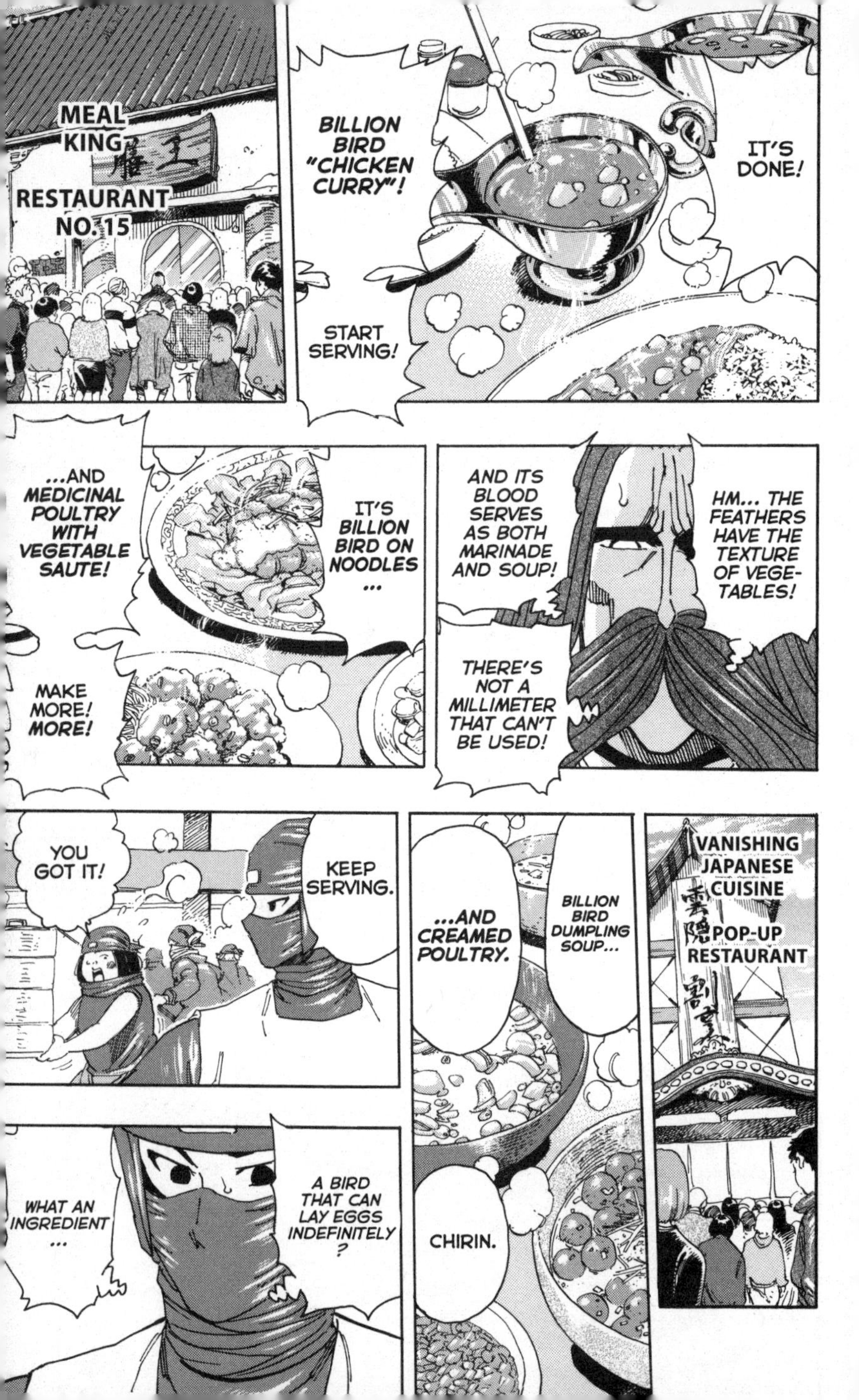
IT'S DONE!
BILLION BIRD "CHICKEN CURRY"!
START SERVING!
MEAL KING
RESTAURANT NO. 15
HM... THE FEATHERS HAVE THE TEXTURE OF VEGE-TABLES!
AND ITS BLOOD SERVES AS BOTH MARINADE AND SOUP!
THERE'S NOT A MILLIMETER THAT CAN'T BE USED!
IT'S BILLION BIRD ON NOODLES...
...AND MEDICINAL POULTRY WITH VEGETABLE SAUTE!
MAKE MORE! MORE!
VANISHING JAPANESE CUISINE
POP-UP RESTAURANT
BILLION BIRD DUMPLING SOUP...
...AND CREAMED POULTRY.
CHIRIN.
KEEP SERVING.
YOU GOT IT!
A BIRD THAT CAN LAY EGGS INDEFINITELY?
WHAT AN INGREDIENT...

OIL KING
OIL KING
FLAGSHIP RESTAURANT
DEEP-FRIED BILLION BIRD!
"CHICKEN NUGGETS" AND "CHICKEN CUTLETS"!
HEARING THE SOUND OF A FRESH INGRE-DIENT FRYING IN OIL AFTER SO LONG...
...MAKES MY HEART DANCE!
IT WAS...
...THE FIRST "REAL INGREDIENT" THE PEOPLE OF THE WORLD HAD TASTED...
...IN ALMOST A YEAR.

MOM!
ISN'T THIS GOOD, MOM?
YES, IT REALLY IS.
YUMMMM!
I'M...
MMPH... MMPH...
...TEARING UP SO MUCH...
...THAT I CAN'T SEE MY FOOD...!
BY NO MEANS...
...WAS BILLION BIRD THE PINNACLE OF CUISINE, BUT...
...THE SMELL OF A REAL FOOD INSTEAD OF A TABLET...
...THE REAL MEAT JUICES THAT GUSHED INSIDE ONE'S MOUTH...
...AND THE TEXTURE THAT ECHOED THROUGHOUT ONE'S BODY WITH EACH BITE...
...REMINDED PEOPLE ONCE AGAIN...
...OF THE JOY OF EATING.
I REALLY GOTTA HAND IT TO THEM.

HAND IT TO WHOM, TORIKO?
THE CURRENT CHEFS OF THE HUMAN WORLD.
THE STUFF THEY'RE COMING UP WITH TASTES MUCH BETTER THAN THE BRAIN DATA I SAMPLED IN GOURMET CASINO.
THEY WERE ALL ABLE TO COOK IT INTO SOMETHING PRETTY PALATABLE.
IS THAT SO?
I...DON'T THINK THAT'S TRUE.
HM?
OH. I DON'T MEAN WHAT YOU SAID ABOUT THE CHEFS.
I JUST NEVER THOUGHT THAT BILLION BIRD WAS THAT BAD TASTING TO START WITH.
IN FACT, I THINK IT'S THE BEST FOOD THERE IS.
I REALLY CAN'T FATHOM WHY IT WENT EXTINCT IN THE PAST.
I GUESS THE CREATURES OF THE PAST COULDN'T UNDERSTAND...
...YOUR TASTE.
MYO
MYO
...
I WONDER...
...WHAT IT FELT LIKE FOR HUNDREDS OF MILLIONS OF YEARS...
...GOING EXTINCT...
...WHILE NO ONE NOTICED.

...
KOMA-TSU...
"NO MATTER HOW AMAZING A FULL-COURSE MEAL YOU PUT TOGETHER..."
"...IT ISN'T WORTH A THING IF THERE ISN'T ANYONE WHO CAN PREPARE IT.
"LIKE MY FULL COURSE."
...
IN THIS AGE...
...EVERYONE'S CALLING YOU...
..."DELICIOUS."
THEY'RE SAYING YOU'RE INCREDIBLY TASTY.
THANK YOU...
...FOR BEING BORN INTO THE WORLD AGAIN.
"WE CAN'T WAIT FOR YOU...
"...TO BE BORN ALIVE AND HEALTHY.
I REALLY...
...REALLY APPRECIATE YOU.
"WE CAN'T WAIT."
PLIP

FLAP
FROOOSH
OH...

HUH ...?!
MYOOOO
WHO
FLAP
OSH
WAH !!

FLAP
FLAP
W... WHAT IN THE?!
THE BILLION BIRD...
...FLEW?!
IT'S NOT SUPPOSED TO BE ABLE TO FLY.
IT JUST...
GLEAM
GLEAM
W...
WHAT...
WHAT BEAUTIFUL FEATHERS!
I'VE NEVER SEEN SUCH BEAUTIFUL WINGS!

...
OLD MAN...
...ARE YOU WATCHING?!
YOUR FULL-COURSE MEAL...
...TOOK FLIGHT!
MYO
MYO
NOW THAT PEOPLE FINALLY APPRECIATE IT...
...IT'S DANCING IN THE BIG BLUE SKY!
AHA! THE BILLION BIRD...
...LOOKS SO HAPPY!
AH!
SQNNNN
POOM

THEY BOTH...
...FELT IT AT THE SAME TIME.
IT WAS STRONGER THAN MERE INTUITION.
IT WAS A CONVICTION!
...
THESE ...
THESE EGGS ...
TORIKO!
I THINK THE BILLION BIRD...
YEAH!
IT'S A FOOD THAT *REQUIRES SPECIAL PREPARATION!*

LET'S TASTE IT FOR OURSELVES WITH THE GUYS!
AND THEN DELIVER THE EGGS ACROSS THE WORLD!
HOTEL GOURMET
OOOH!
THAT UGLY BILLION BIRD FLEW?!
AND IT WAS BEAUTIFUL TO BEHOLD ?!
BUT IT HAD SUCH A NASTY FACE!
IT'S TRUE!
AND IT HAD A CUTE FACE.
MORE IMPORT-ANTLY, THESE EGGS...
... WEREN'T LAID AFTER A THREAT.
THEY'RE THE FIRST EGGS LAID AFTER PRAISE.
HOW CURIOUS ...
LET'S DIG IN, EVERYONE!
YEAH!
KRK
KRK

KRAK
PLOP
OOH! CHECK IT OUT, IT'S NOT SPILLING OVER.
IT'S SUPER SPRINGY.
IT'S KINDA LIKE A CLEAR PUDDING.
HM ...?
THERE'S NO YOLK ...?
ACTUALLY, IF YOU LOOK CLOSELY, YOU CAN SEE THE YOLK IS DIFFUSED THROUGHOUT.
LIKE AN EGG INLAID WITH GOLD DUST.
LET'S EAT ALREADY!
ALL RIGHT THEN! TIME TO EAT...
... BILLION BIRD EGG!
WOW ...
SLUP

SHOOP
OH ...!
OOH ...
IN A FLASH, THE INSIDE OF MY MOUTH--
FRSH
OOOOOOOH!!
HNNG
FRSH
DWUH?! TORIKO?!
FWUSH
...
GULP

TAK
HFF
HFF
D...
YOUR HAIR GREW, TORIKO!
W... WHAT?!
DELICIOUS!!
IT WAS SO GOOD THAT EVERYTHING GREW.
JUST LIKE IN THE GOURMET WORLD.
THE BILLION BIRD LIVES FOR HUNDREDS OF MILLIONS OF YEARS...
...AND YOU CAN TASTE THOSE YEARS LAYERED LIKE THICK STRATA.
THAT FLAVOR BLEW THROUGH MY BODY IN AN INSTANT!

YUMMMM!!
ZWANG
SUNNY, YOUR EYELASHES ARE CRAZY!
AT FIRSTS IT SEEMS LIKE A STARCHY SYRUP...
BUT IT SLIPS SMOOTHLY INTO THE MOUTH.
...OR MORE LIKE A THICK, STICKY SWEET SOUP.
ET TU, COCO?!
IF THAT IS COCO...
HM... IT'S LESS LIKE AN EGG...AND MORE LIKE A DRINK.
ZEBRA TOO!
YOU'RE ONE TO TALK, KOMATSU!
HUH?
THEY FEEL CLEAN AND REFRESHED...
FORGET ALL THAT.
...LIKE THEY'VE JUST BEEN WASHED.
MY STOMACH...
MY HEART...
IT'S LIKE MY BODY, ON A GENETIC LEVEL...
...DOWN TO EVERY MICROSCOPIC INJURY, WAS REPAIRED.
I FEEL FRESH AND YOUNG AGAIN!
HEY, KOMATSU.
YES, TORIKO.
KRK
THE MOMENT THESE EGGS WERE LAID...
...WE'D ALREADY DECIDED IT.

KRAK
JIGJUUB
FLASH
BILLION BIRD EGG
A TOAST!
TO THIS FOOD.
IT'S ALL RIGHT, ISN'T IT?
OLD MAN...

I'M MAKING BILLION BIRD EGG...
TORIKO'S FULL-COURSE MEAL
BB CORN
CENTURY SOUP
ENTREE
SALAD
DESSERT
RAINBOW FRUIT
DRINK
BILLION BIRD EGG
...THE DRINK IN MY FULL-COURSE MEAL!
TORIKO! ♡
ABOUT THE PROGRAM FOR THE WEDDING ...
WHAT'S GOING ON?!
YOU ALL LOOK LIKE GIRLS!

TORIKO

GOURMET CHECKLIST

Vol. 292

DURIAN BOMB
(FRUIT)

CAPTURE LEVEL: 68

HABITAT: SMELLY PLACES

SIZE: 3 METERS

HEIGHT: ---

WEIGHT: 4.5 TONS

PRICE: 0–40,000,000 YEN (FOR 1 HOUR)

SCALE

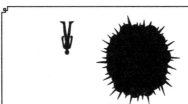

THE WORLD'S STINKIEST FOOD. ALSO GOES BY THE NAME OF "STINK BOMB." THERE ARE RECORDS OF DURIAN BOMB BEING USED AS A WEAPON IN ANCIENT WARS, AND IT'S SO DANGEROUSLY ODORIFIC THAT THE IGO LIMITS ITS CIRCULATION. THE RIPER IT BECOMES, THE MORE DELICIOUS IT BECOMES TOO...AND ALSO THE NASTIER IT SMELLS. SO THOUGH ITS SMELL IS ATROCIOUS, RIPE DURIAN BOMB IS A FLAVOR BOMB IN THE KITCHEN. IT WAS AN IMPORTANT INGREDIENT IN THE FORTUNE ROLL THAT MONCHY PREPARED FOR DIVINING THE LOCATION OF CHOWLIN TEMPLE.

GOURMET 269: INHERITED SPIRIT!!

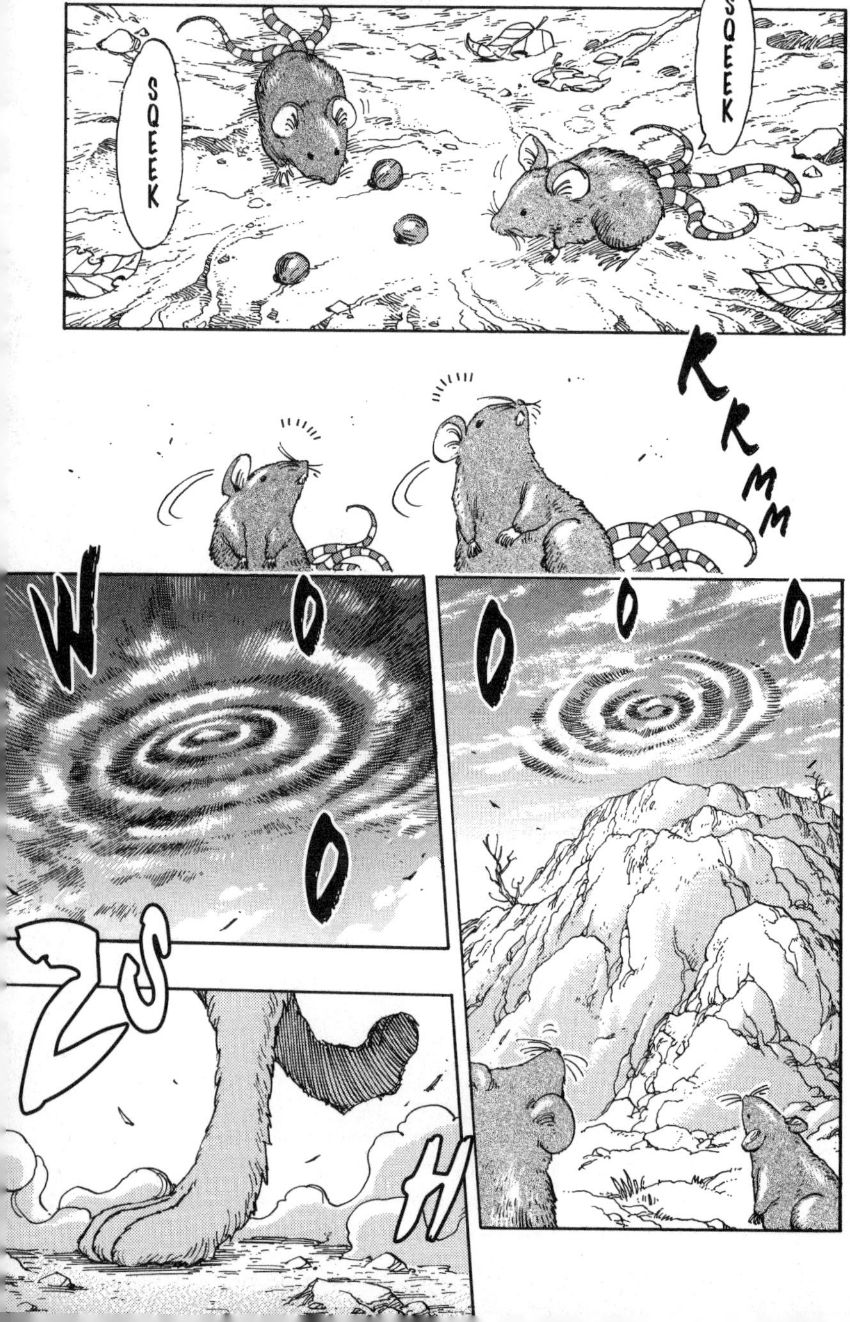

WOOO
GOURMET 269: INHERITED SPIRIT!!

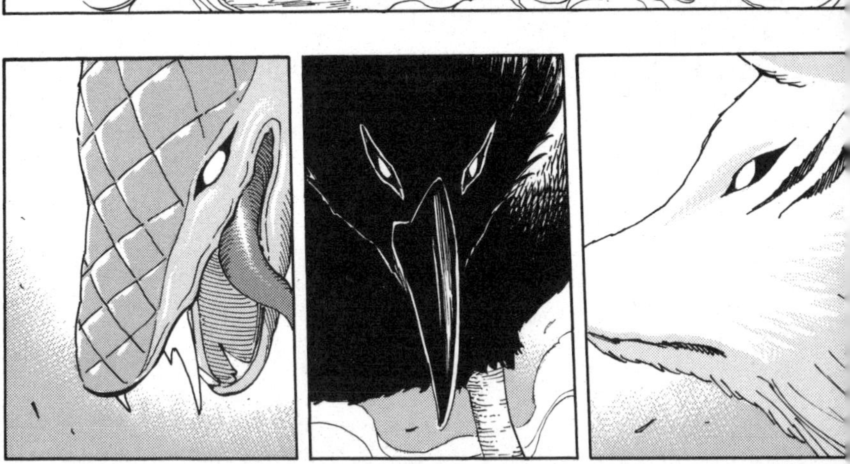

BSS
SHT
ZWAN
G!!
ZSH
SKI-D-D
SS
LS

OOOOOM

I'M BACK ...
TERRY!
DOMF
SORRY I TOOK SO LONG, TERRY.
AROO
HA HA!
I KNOW I WORRIED YOU, BUT...
...IT'S GOING TO BE ALL RIGHT NOW.

FROM NOW ON, LET'S HUNT TOGETHER AGAIN.
ALWAYS TO-GETHER.
SO YOU, KISS AND QUINN ARE ALL TRAINING TOGETHER, HUH?
LOOKS LIKE EVERYONE'S READY TO ENTER THE *GOURMET WORLD.*
TORIKO!
YO!
GOURMET
TOM!

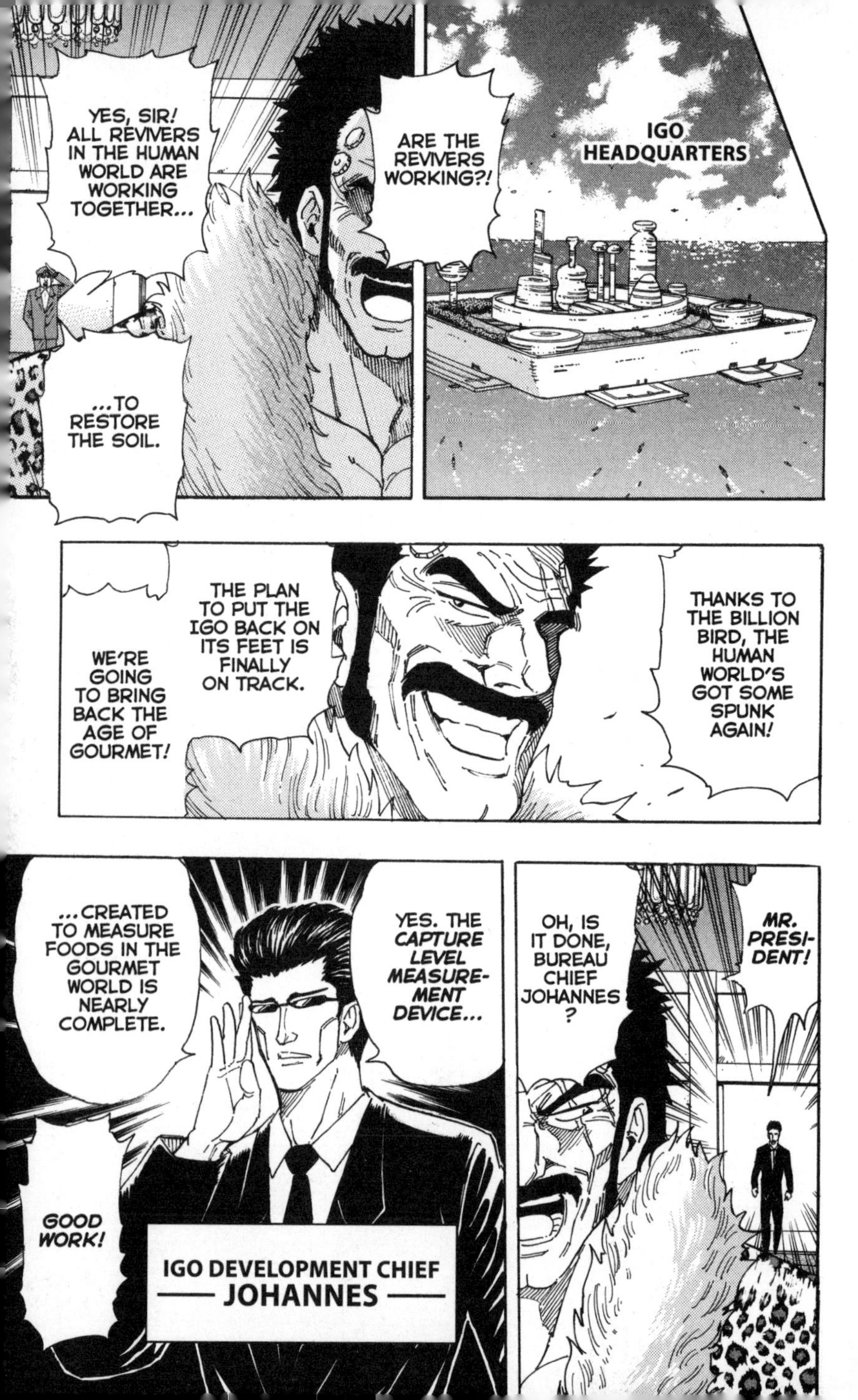
IGO HEADQUARTERS
ARE THE REVIVERS WORKING?!
YES, SIR! ALL REVIVERS IN THE HUMAN WORLD ARE WORKING TOGETHER...
...TO RESTORE THE SOIL.
THANKS TO THE BILLION BIRD, THE HUMAN WORLD'S GOT SOME SPUNK AGAIN!
THE PLAN TO PUT THE IGO BACK ON ITS FEET IS FINALLY ON TRACK.
WE'RE GOING TO BRING BACK THE AGE OF GOURMET!
MR. PRESI-DENT!
OH, IS IT DONE, BUREAU CHIEF JOHANNES?
YES. THE CAPTURE LEVEL MEASURE-MENT DEVICE...
...CREATED TO MEASURE FOODS IN THE GOURMET WORLD IS NEARLY COMPLETE.
GOOD WORK!
IGO DEVELOPMENT CHIEF
— JOHANNES —

WE OWE IT ALL TO THE BILLION BIRD.
I KNEW IT. FOODS FROM THE GOURMET WORLD REALLY ARE INDISPENSABLE TO RESTORING THE AGE OF GOURMET!
AND TO GET THEM ...
...WE'RE GOING TO NEED THE STRENGTH OF *THOSE* *FOUR.*
...
STILL, I CAN'T BELIEVE ...
...THIS EGG MADE IT INTO TORIKO'S FULL-COURSE MEAL.
CLINK
PRESI-DENT ICHIRYU ...
I HOPE YOU'RE SMILING RIGHT NOW.
BACK THEN, WHEN THE PREZ TOOK IN TORIKO...
...I GUESS IT REALLY WASN'T A WRONG MOVE.

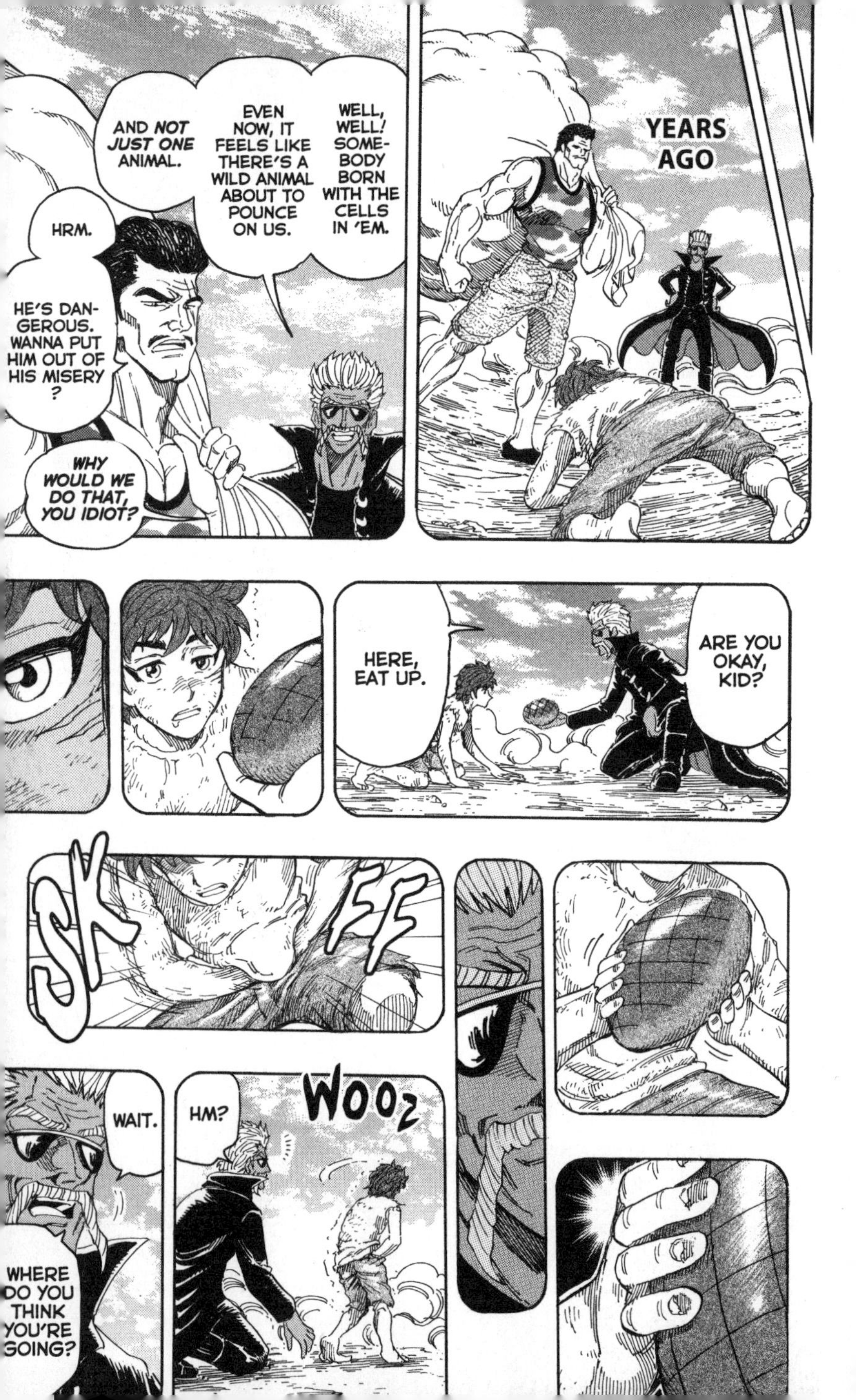
YEARS AGO
WELL, WELL! SOMEBODY BORN WITH THE CELLS IN 'EM.
EVEN NOW, IT FEELS LIKE THERE'S A WILD ANIMAL ABOUT TO POUNCE ON US.
AND NOT JUST ONE ANIMAL.
HRM.
HE'S DANGEROUS. WANNA PUT HIM OUT OF HIS MISERY?
WHY WOULD WE DO THAT, YOU IDIOT?
ARE YOU OKAY, KID?
HERE, EAT UP.
SKFF
WOOZ
HM?
WAIT.
WHERE DO YOU THINK YOU'RE GOING?

...
I'M GOING TO...
...MY VILLAGE ...
THANK YOU VERY MUCH ...
...FOR THE BREAD. IT MEANS A LOT...
EVERYBODY IN THE VILLAGE... IS SO HUNGRY...
I'M GONNA BRING THEM...
...THIS BREAD...
WE'LL ALL...
WOOZE
... SPLIT IT...
...AND EAT... TO... GETHER ...
WOOZE
ALL OF ...
... US ...
...
THIS KID...
...
HE ONLY HAS NUBS OF NAILS.
IT'S A SIGN THAT HE'S BEEN BITING THEM.

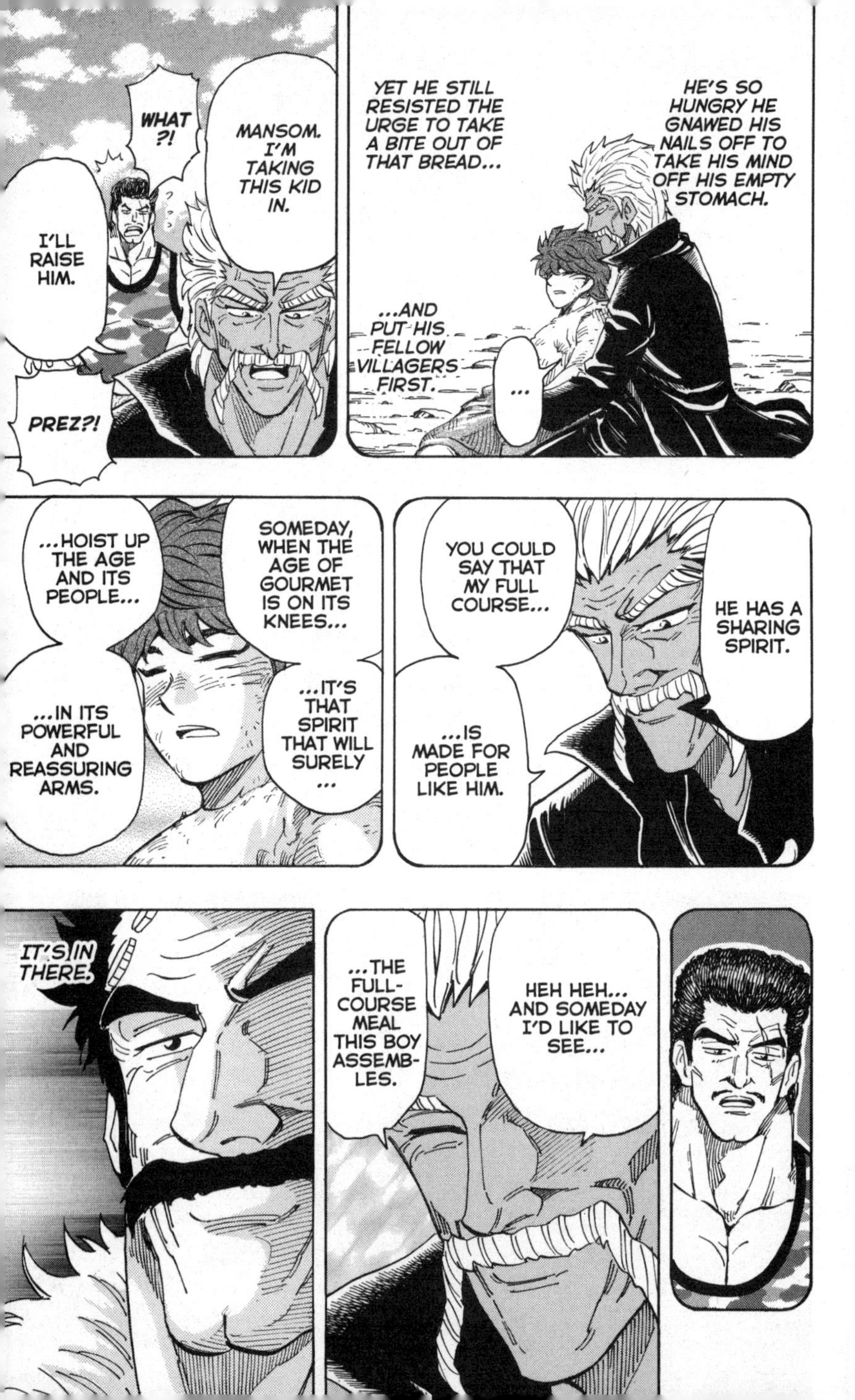
HE'S SO HUNGRY HE GNAWED HIS NAILS OFF TO TAKE HIS MIND OFF HIS EMPTY STOMACH.
YET HE STILL RESISTED THE URGE TO TAKE A BITE OUT OF THAT BREAD...
...AND PUT HIS FELLOW VILLAGERS FIRST.
...
MANSOM. I'M TAKING THIS KID IN.
WHAT?!
I'LL RAISE HIM.
PREZ?!
HE HAS A SHARING SPIRIT.
YOU COULD SAY THAT MY FULL COURSE...
...IS MADE FOR PEOPLE LIKE HIM.
SOMEDAY, WHEN THE AGE OF GOURMET IS ON ITS KNEES...
...IT'S THAT SPIRIT THAT WILL SURELY ...
...HOIST UP THE AGE AND ITS PEOPLE...
...IN ITS POWERFUL AND REASSURING ARMS.
HEH HEH... AND SOMEDAY I'D LIKE TO SEE...
...THE FULL-COURSE MEAL THIS BOY ASSEMB-LES.
IT'S IN THERE.

THE PREZ'S HOPES AND IDEALS...
...ARE IN TORIKO'S FULL-COURSE MEAL.

GOURMET WORLD
CAPE OF FOOD'S END
OH, THAT'S IT.
LITTLE ICHI'S APPETIZ-ER.
THE MILLION TREE.
MIDORA PLANTED THIS INSTEAD OF A TOMBSTONE.
...
IT'S GROWN SO TALL AND STRONG.
AND ALL THESE *FOOD'S END FLOWERS* ARE IN FULL BLOOM.
EVEN THOUGH I'VE HEARD THIS REGION HAS BEEN DRY AND BARREN FOR AGES.
DID A REVIVER DO THIS?
NO.
IT'S PROBABLY MIDORA'S WORK TOO.
MIDORA'S ...?

THAT GUY...
...STOLE ICHI'S SKILL.
CAPE OF FOOD'S END IS FULL OF MEMORIES FROM WHEN THE THREE OF US TRAINED.
MIDORA WAS A MEEK LITTLE KID BACK THEN.
BUT NOW, HE'S PROBABLY MORE THAN I CAN HANDLE.
GLUB GLUB
JUST FORGET ABOUT THAT NINNY.
SOONER OR LATER HE'LL END UP PAYING FOR THE MESS HE MADE OF THE HUMAN WORLD.
WHAT MATTERS RIGHT NOW IS *JOIE.*
GUESS YOU AND I WILL HAVE TO...
...FIGHT 'EM HEAD ON.
THE EARTH ...
...THE VERY PLANET...
...IS SHIFTING VIOLENTLY.
THIS HAS NEVER HAPPENED BEFORE.

"NIGHT" IS FALLING ON THE GOURMET WORLD.
WE WON'T BE ABLE TO MOVE FREELY ANYMORE.
OUR LAST DAYS MIGHT BE SPENT HERE IN THE GOURMET WORLD, JIRO.
YEAH, WELL... WE'LL JUST DO WHAT WE CAN.
JUST YOU WAIT, ICHI...
TILL I CAN JOIN YOU FOR A DRINK ON THE OTHER SIDE.
FOR NOW, WE'LL WAIT FOR TORIKO AND THE OTHERS HERE IN THE GOURMET WORLD.
WE'LL PROBABLY NEVER RETURN TO THE HUMAN WORLD.
WILL THE HUMAN WORLD ...
... BE OKAY, SETSU?
IT'LL BE FINE.
THOSE YOUNGSTERS ARE STRONGER ...
...THAN WE GIVE THEM CREDIT FOR.

HUMAN WORLD
SETSUNO'S DINER
I SEE...
SO CHEF SETSUNO'S GONE TO THE GOURMET WORLD.
YES.
SHE DIDN'T SAY WHEN SHE'D BE BACK.
UM...
NONO, WAS IT?
UH...
Y... YES.
THE HUMAN WORLD MAY BE IN THIS AWFUL STATE NOW, BUT...
...WE REMAINING CHEFS HAVE TO DO WHAT WE CAN AND NOT GIVE UP!
YES!
WELL, I'LL COME BACK ANOTHER TIME!
OH!
CHEF KOMA-TSU!

YES?
UH... WELL ...
CHEF KOMATSU ...
... ARE YOU GOING BACK TO THE GOURMET WORLD TOO?
!
YES!
I AM!
I...I SEE...
YEP!
ALONG WITH TORIKO AND EVERYONE!
UM... IF IT'D BE ALL RIGHT, CHEF KOMATSU... WOULD YOU CARE FOR A MEAL?
SINCE YOU CAME ALL THE WAY TO SETSUNO'S DINER AND ALL...
HUH?
YES! YOU CAN EAT ALL YOU WANT!
ALL WE HAVE IS THE BILLION BIRD THAT YOU SUPPLIED US, BUT...
CAN I?!
WOW, I CAN'T BELIEVE CHEF SETSUNO'S PUPIL...
...IS GOING TO SERVE ME A MEAL!
It's a dream come true!
ME TOO! IT'S AN HONOR TO HAVE CHEF KOMATSU TASTE MY COOKING!
TSU NO'S DINER

KLAK
CHEERS!
IT'S KIND OF A PLAIN BEER FOR YOUR SEND-OFF PARTY, BUT...
NO, IT'S FINE!
GOOD JOB FINDING SOME, TOM!
I KEPT IT HIDDEN FOR WHEN YOU CAME BACK.
SO YOU'RE TAKING OFF RIGHT AWAY?
YEP.
BUT BE-FORE I DO...
...THERE'S SOMEBODY I HAVE TO TALK TO FIRST.
...
IN ANY CASE, THIS NEXT TRIP IS GOING TO BE A PRETTY LONG ONE.
I DON'T EVEN KNOW IF I'LL BE COMING BACK TO THE HUMAN WORLD AGAIN.
I'M GOING TO REST UP SO THAT I CAN BE AT MY BEST.
NICE.
ALL YOU GUYS OUGHT TO TAKE IT EASY BEFORE YOU LEAVE...

YOU'RE THE STRONGEST ...
...THE HUMAN WORLD HAS TO OFFER.

TORIKO

GOURMET CHECKLIST

Vol. 293

ECO SEAWEED
(SKIN)

CAPTURE LEVEL: 15
HABITAT: ECO LAND
SIZE: ---
HEIGHT: ---
WEIGHT: ---
PRICE: 1M^2 PIECE / 800,000 YEN

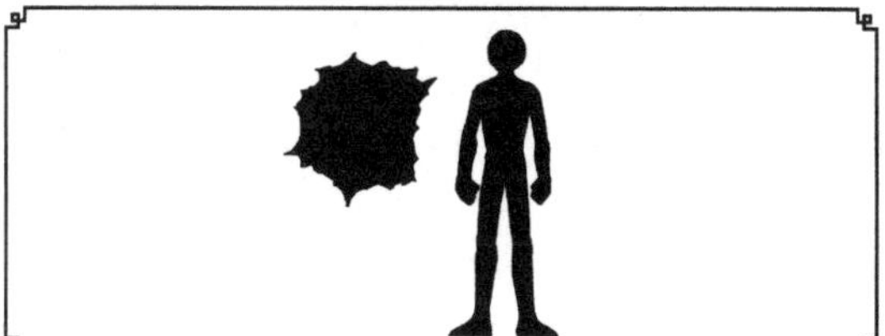

SCALE

A SEAWEED YOU CAN PEEL OFF THE SHELLS OF SOLAR TURTLES LIVING IN ECO LAND, A VILLAGE ON HUMBLE FARE HILL. THE SOLAR TURTLE'S SHELL IS MADE OF NATURALLY OCCURRING SOLAR PANELS WITH THE LITTLE-UNDERSTOOD ABILITY TO CONVERT SUNLIGHT INTO ELECTRICITY. WHEN THE SOLAR TURTLE'S SHELL'S CHARGE IS LOW, YOU CAN PEEL OFF A THIN LAYER OF ITS SHELL. THAT'S ECO SEAWEED. IT'S MORE THAN EDIBLE, AND IS CONSIDERED A HIGH-CLASS WRAPPING FOR RICE BALLS. HENCE WHY IT WAS AN IMPORTANT INGREDIENT IN THE FORTUNE ROLL THAT MONCHY PREPARED FOR DIVINING THE LOCATION OF CHOWLIN TEMPLE.

HEY, YOU FIVE!!
EVERYTHING READY?!
ZSSH
FOR ENTERING HELL--THE GOURMET WORLD!!
YEAH!
GOURMET 270: THE FINAL KEY!!
GOOD. THEN GET GOING.
SNAP TO IT.
LAZY!!
WHY ARE YOU ACTING SO FANCY?!
YOU THINK YOU'RE HOT STUFF NOW?

GOURMET 270: THE FINAL KEY!!

THAT'S RIGHT.
I FIGURED IF THERE WAS SOMEONE WHO COULD GIVE US INFORMA-TION...
...THEN WE'D BETTER GO AND ASK THEM RIGHT AWAY.
IN EVERY BIOTOPE, EACH OF THE TREASURE CHESTS...
HUH? BUT THERE WASN'T ANYTHING IN BIOTOPE 1, WAS THERE?
MWSH
ACTUAL-LY...
...WAS PROTECTED BY A CREATURE.
WE COULDN'T GATHER THE OLD MAN'S FULL-COURSE MEAL WITHOUT DEFEATING THEM.

THERE IS.
IN HERE.
WHAT A PAIN.
LET'S JUST GET THIS OVER WITH.
HWOO
WAIT! WHAT'RE YOU GOING TO DO, ZEBRA?!
VOICE CUTTER

SHH
LA
WHAT?!
IT DIDN'T EVEN LEAVE A SCRATCH!

SO THIS IS A TREE THAT MY VOICE CUTTER CAN'T CUT?
IT'S A GOURMET WORLD TREE...
IT HAS TO BE IF IT'S THAT TOUGH.
QUIT BEING SO VIOLENT. THERE'S AN ENTRANCE.
IT'S ON THE THIRD FLOOR.
CHAK
HELLO, IS ANYBODY HOME?
OH, WOW!
EVERYTHING IN THE HOUSE IS MADE OUT OF LEAVES.

EVEN THIS REFRIGERATOR'S MADE OUT OF LEAVES.
PWAF
WOW, IT'S JUST LIKE A GOURMET CASE.
IS THIS THE LIBRARY, I WONDER?
UH ...
THE MANIA
HOT STUFF
780 YEN
WHAT'S WITH ALL THESE DIRTY MAGS?
WE CAN GO DOWN THIS WAY!
JUST WHAT KIND OF PERSON LIVES HERE?
OH, THE SECOND FLOOR'S THE BEDROOM.
THERE'S NOBODY HERE.
I GUESS THEY'RE THE NEXT FLOOR DOWN.
MORE DIRTY MAGS... OH, AND COOKBOOKS...

HUH?
THERE'S NO STAIRWAY LEADING DOWN.
YOU'RE RIGHT. THERE'S NO STEPS.
MAYBE THEY'RE HIDING...
...UNDERNEATH HERE?
OH, WELL.
IT'S A LITTLE OVERKILL, BUT...
GRRK
...I'LL JUST HAVE TO BUST IN.
GRRK
NAIL GUN

BAAM
WAH!
AAH!
OH!
IT DIDN'T BUDGE.
EVEN THOUGH I REALLY RAMPED THAT UP.
OUTTA THE WAY.
H-WOO
ACK! ZEBRA, DON'T ...!

SOUND BAZOOKA!!
ZW
AA
TH...
WOOOO
THAT'S SOME TREE.
HOW ARE WE SUPPOSED TO GET IN?
NO MISTAKING IT, THERE'S A FIRST FLOOR.
MY NOSE TELLS ME SO.

FRSH
!
SUNNY ?!
THIS IS JUST ANOTHER OF THE PRESIDENT'S PRANKS.
HE UNDER-ESTIMATES US.
DINING KITCHEN
THERE MUST BE SOME WAY IN.
GROPE
GROPE
I'LL SEARCH EVERY NOOK AND CRANNY OF THIS AREA TO FIND IT.
HMMM?
THERE'S SOME-THING...
...FISHY ABOUT THAT WELL.
HEY! THERE ARE STEPS IN HERE!
BINGO !!

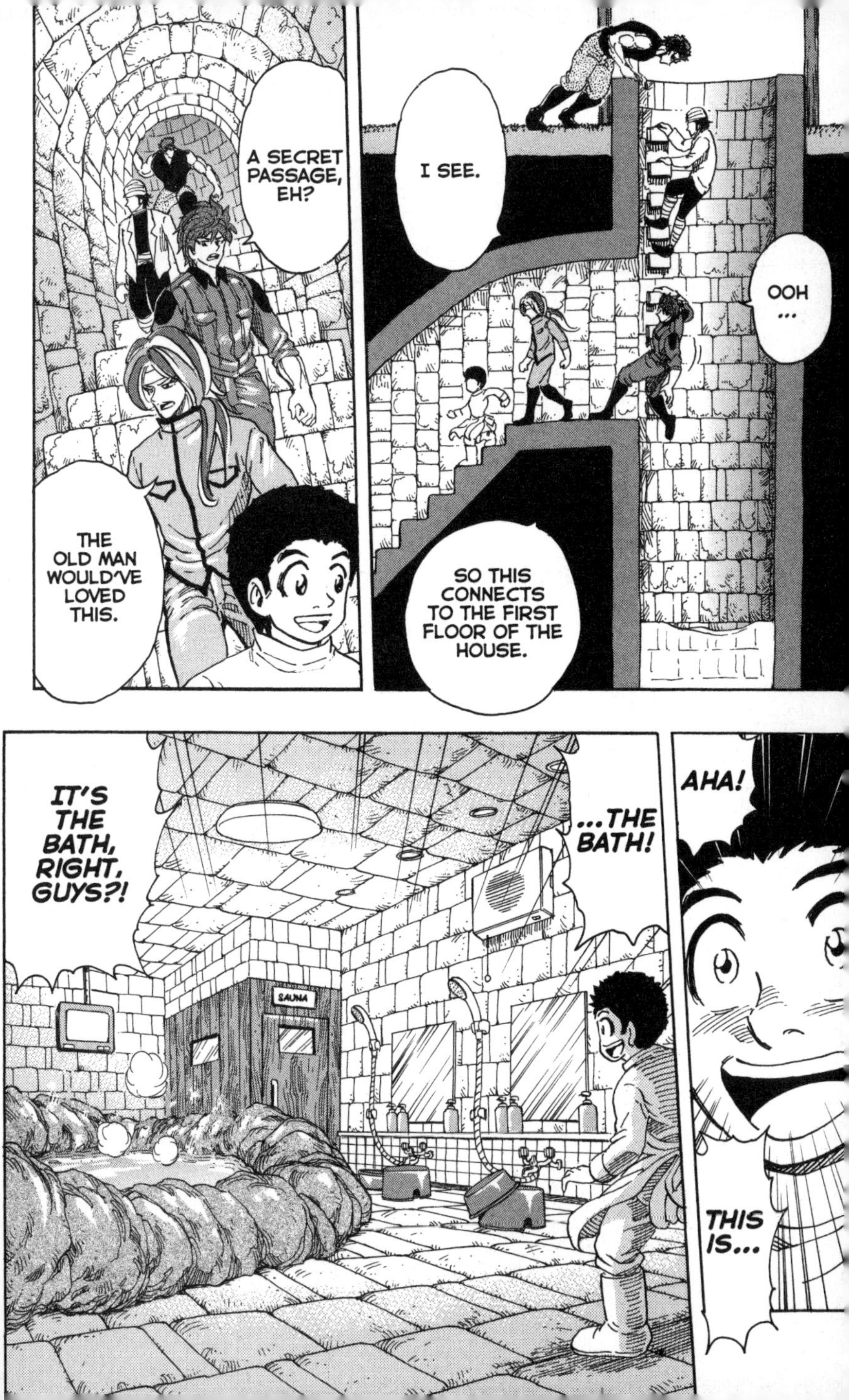
OOH ...
I SEE.
SO THIS CONNECTS TO THE FIRST FLOOR OF THE HOUSE.
A SECRET PASSAGE, EH?
THE OLD MAN WOULD'VE LOVED THIS.
AHA!
THIS IS...
...THE BATH!
IT'S THE BATH, RIGHT, GUYS?!
SAUNA

SAUNA
WOW, WHAT A HUGE UNDER-GROUND BATHHOUSE!
AND IT'S A NATURAL HOT SPRING, ISN'T IT?!
LET'S TAKE A DIP!
YES! LET'S!
THAT'S NOT...
...WHAT WE'RE HERE FOR.
THE ELECTRO-MAGNETIC WAVES I'VE PICKED UP...
...TELL ME SOME-THING'S NOT QUITE RIGHT ABOUT THIS POND.
IT LEADS SOME-WHERE.
I'LL DIVE IN AND TAKE A LOOK.
SPLASH

BLOOP
BLOOP
BLOOP
BLOOP
BLOOP
SPLASH
...

SO THE POND'S CONNECTED TO THE WELL.
I ALREADY KNEW THAT THANKS TO MY ECHO-LOCATION.
THEN YOU SHOULD'VE TOLD ME SOONER, ZEBRA.
UH-OH, COCO'S ELECTRO-MAGNETIC WAVES AREN'T UP TO SNUFF.
ARE YOU LOSING YOUR ACCU-RACY?
HUH?
THIS FIRST-FLOOR WINDOW OPENS NORMALLY.
TUNK
WHAAAT?! IT DOES?!
BAM
IT WAS STARING US RIGHT IN THE FACE THIS WHOLE TIME.
ACK!
YOU MAKIN' FUN OF US?!
OKAY, OKAY. LET'S GO IN.
TMP

...
WHA...
WHAT THE HECK ?!
IS IT...
...A GT ROBOT ?!
NO, THAT THING'S ALIVE!
WAIT, THEN...
IT'S A NITRO?!
IT'S IN HIBER-NATION!
WATER!
BRING WATER!
...
I'M AWAKE !!
SMACK
HUH ...?

SPURT
SIT DOWN! ALL OF YOU!
BUT FIRST LINE UP! AT ATTENTION!
HUH?
HUH ?!
I'M SO HOPPING MAD, I'M ABOUT READY TO POP!
NOW LOOK HERE!
I'VE GOT ABOUT A HUNDRED THINGS TO TELL YOU GUYS, SO SIT DOWN!
WHAT TOOK YOU SO DAMN LONG?!
BUT FIRST A SMACK!
AND YOU CUT MY HEAD WHEN YOU BUSTED IN MY WINDOW!
I'M GONNA SMACK YOU FIRST!
WE CAN'T START UNTIL I DO!
W-W-WAIT...
WAIT A SECOND ...!
WH...WHO IN THE WORLD...
...ARE YOU?!
WHAAAAAT?!
WHO AM I?!
WHO AM I, YOU ASK?!
erk!
YOU...
YOU'RE UNBELIEV-ABLE...

YOU REALLY HAVEN'T HEARD OF ME?
NOPE.
LITTLE ICHI, YOU WERE SUP-POSED TO TELL THEM!
TELL THEM FIRST THING!
AAH
"LITTLE ICHI"?
HM... FINE... SO YOU KNOW ABOUT ICHIRYU.
WELL, I'M CHICHI THE FLAVOR HERMIT!
ICHIRYU'S PARTNER!
ACTUALLY, THAT PART ABOUT BEING PARTNERS WAS A LIE.
WHAAAAAAT?!
WHAAAAAT?!

TORIKO

GOURMET CHECKLIST

Vol. 294

ECO ECO SKUNK
(MAMMAL)

CAPTURE LEVEL: 2

HABITAT: ECO LAND

SIZE: 50 CM

HEIGHT: ---

WEIGHT: 3 KG

PRICE: 1 CUBIC METER OF GAS / 3,000 YEN

AN ECO ECO SKUNK!
THE GAS COMES FROM ITS FARTS.
POOT
POOT
HUH? WHAT KIND OF ANIMAL IS THAT?!

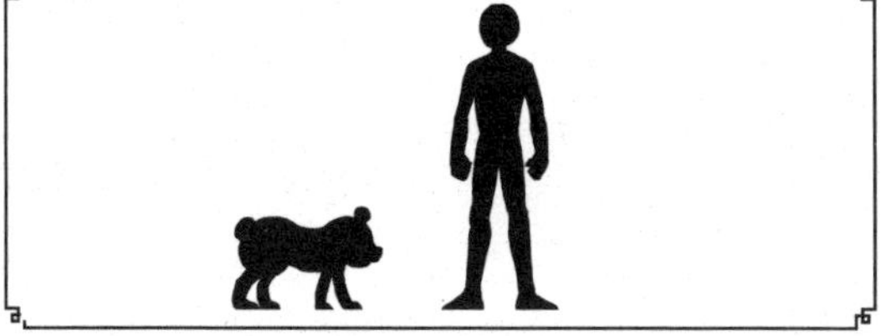

SCALE

A MAMMAL IN THE WEASEL FAMILY. AN ECO ECO SKUNK'S GUT CONJURES UP SOME PRETTY UNIQUE GAS, RELEASED AS FARTS. ITS FLATULENCE CAN BE USED IN A HOME JUST LIKE MUNICIPAL GAS, ONLY MORE ECOLOGICAL AND CONVENIENT. ECO ECO SKUNK ISN'T SUITABLE FOR CONSUMPTION, BUT PEOPLE ARE HOPING TO SPREAD IT BEYOND ECO LAND TO REDUCE GAS BILLS AND HELP THE ENVIRONMENT.

I GUESS I'LL HAVE TO EXPLAIN IN DETAIL...
...MY RELATIONSHIP WITH LITTLE ICHI.
I DON'T REMEMBER WHEN WE FIRST MET...
AT THE TIME, I'D BEEN HIBERNATING FOR MANY THOUSANDS OF YEARS.
...BUT I'D SAY IT WAS ABOUT 500 YEARS AGO.
GLUB
GLUB
THE ONE WHO AWOKE ME WAS...
...LITTLE ICHI.
AND THEN... WELL...
HERE I AM NOW.
WHAT ABOUT IN BETWEEN ?!
YOU LEFT OUT WAY TOO MUCH!
SIP
LIKE ALL THE INFO!
OH, I'M SORRY. IT WASN'T 500 YEARS AGO. WE MET MORE LIKE 490 YEARS AGO.
THAT PART DOESN'T MATTER!
At all!
WAIT, NO...I THINK IT WAS 480 YEARS AGO.
WE NEED MORE DETAILS!
GOURMET 271: ICHIRYU'S MESSAGE!!

GOURMET 271: ICHIRYU'S MESSAGE!!

WHEN YOU GUYS FOUND THE TREASURE CHEST OUTSIDE, I KNEW YOU REALIZED I WAS IN HERE, BUT...
PLRK
...I CHOSE TO STAY IN HERE, PRETENDING TO HIBERNATE IN ORDER TO SURPRISE YOU.
ANYWAY.
CHAK
TORIKO! LET'S GET GOING ALREADY!
RIGHT.
AWWW!
THEY'RE GONNA IGNORE ME?
I WAS SO SHOCKED, I SWEAR...
WELL, IT'S A GOOD THING YOU MADE IT IN TIME.

PLISH
PLSH
DOINK
VOOP
VOOP
THESE ARE SEAT LEAVES. SIT DOWN.
FIRST SIT, THEN WE TALK.
COMPLETING THE OLD MAN'S FULL-COURSE MEAL WAS MY TOP PRIORITY.
AND... BESIDES ...
D... DON'T MIND IF I DO...
YOU KNOW... I DIDN'T HAVE A CHOICE BACK THEN.
...I FIGURED IT'D BE A PAIN TO DEAL WITH YOU.
YOU GAVE OFF THAT SUSPICIOUS VIBE.
THAT'S WHAT I'M TALKING ABOUT!
YOU'RE NOT TAKING ME SERIOUSLY!
YOU DIDN'T EVEN BRING SO MUCH AS A SLICE OF CAKE!
DO YOU KNOW WHO I AM?!
OH... SORRY WE DIDN'T BRING SOMETHING OVER WHEN WE CAME TO VISIT.
REALLY SORRY.
HMPH!
AS FOR YOU!
WHAT'S YOUR DEAL? YOU SMELL OF FEMALE.
YOU MET WITH A FEMALE BEFORE COMING HERE, DIDN'T YOU?

UH...FEMALE? Y...YEAH, I DID. I MET WITH NONO FROM SETSUNO'S DINER.
LOOK AT THIS!
YOUR CLOTHES ARE STEEPED IN HER SMELL!
YOUNG!
THIS IS THE SMELL OF A YOUNG FEMALE!
HA!
I GUESS NONO'S PRETTY YOUNG...
MAYBE AROUND TWENTY?
PLEASE GIVE ME...
...YOUR CLOTHES.
HUH?!
WHY?!
WHAT'S WITH THAT FACE?
WON'T YOU? IN PLACE OF CAKE?
GIMME THE CLOTHES FIRST.
OTHERWISE I DON'T THINK I'M GOING TO TELL YOU ANYTHING.
NOPE... NOT A THING.
I DON'T REALLY GET THIS, BUT TAKE OFF YOUR CLOTHES, KOMATSU!
HUUUH?
HNNGH!!
I LOVE THEM!
I FEEL A HUNDRED MILLION YEARS YOUNGER! ♡
WHAT THE HECK IS WITH THIS GUY?
HUG
HUG

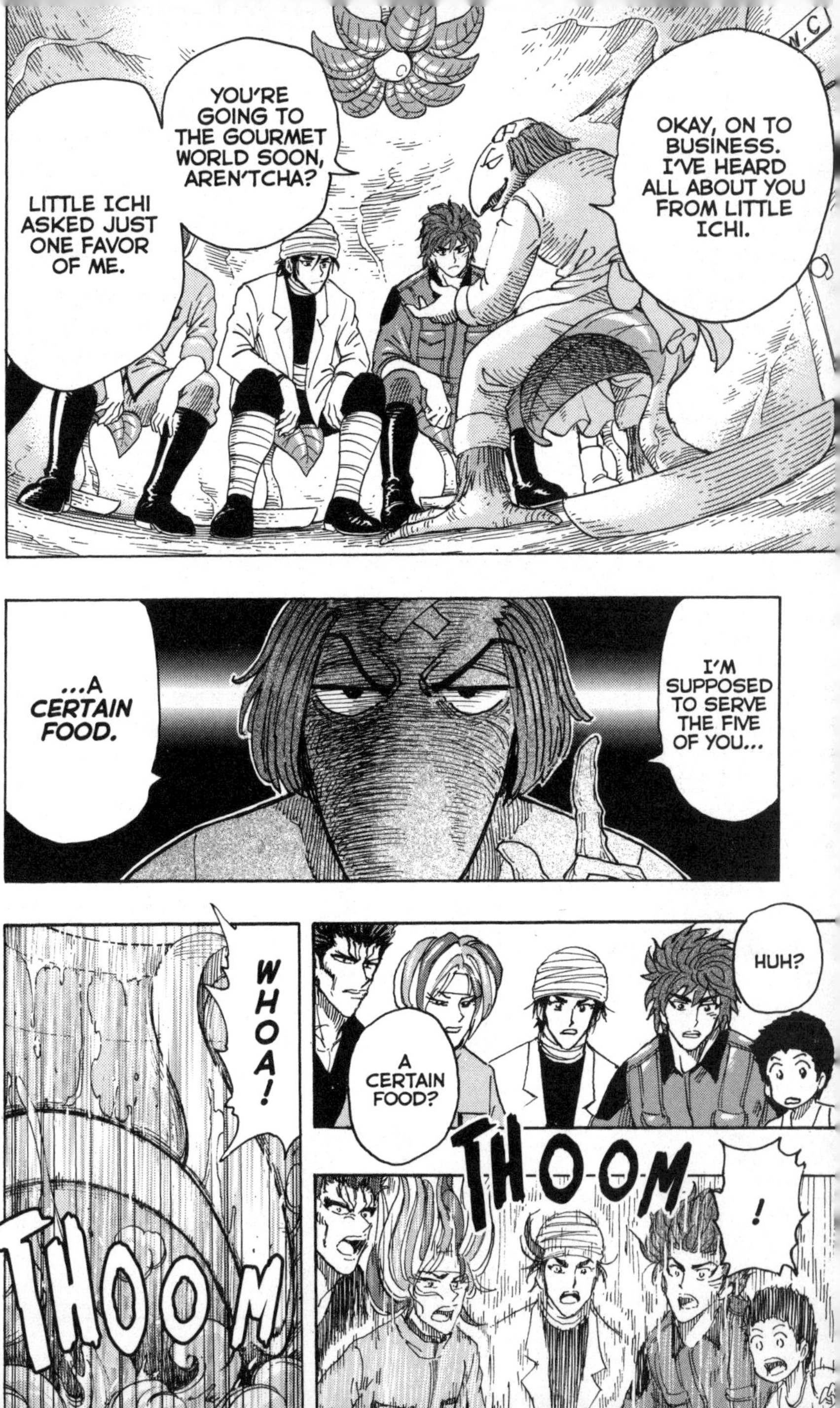
OKAY, ON TO BUSINESS. I'VE HEARD ALL ABOUT YOU FROM LITTLE ICHI.
YOU'RE GOING TO THE GOURMET WORLD SOON, AREN'TCHA?
LITTLE ICHI ASKED JUST ONE FAVOR OF ME.
I'M SUPPOSED TO SERVE THE FIVE OF YOU...
...A CERTAIN FOOD.
HUH?
A CERTAIN FOOD?
WHOA!
THOOM
!
THOOM

...
TH... THAT SCARED ME!
WHERE ARE WE...?
THIS IS MY KITCHEN.
THE FOOD I'M GOING TO SERVE YOU IS...
THAT!
!

UH...
BA DUMP!!
I'M HAVING AN...
UU... AAA AH
HUH ?!
...AUTOMATIC REFLEX!
NO!!

AAA...A
TRYING TO STOP THE REACTION IS TAKING ALL MY ENERGY!
HN
NAH
CAN'T EVEN THINK!
GWA...A
G... GUYS?!
KRIK
HERE COME THE APPETITE DEMONS!!
YAHOO! THEY SHOWED THEMSELVES!
WAH HA HA!

PIPE DOWN, YOU BEASTS !!
ZAZAZASH!
CHK
!!
YOU CAN'T CONTROL YOUR-SELVES AT ALL!
YOU LITTLE CHICKS!
GA HA HA HA
HOW ADORABLE! YOU AUTOMATICALLY REVEALED YOUR TRUE SELVES!

HA HA HA
...
CH... CHICHI ...
CHICHI!!
HM?
WH... WHAT'S GOING ON HERE?!
WHAT ON EARTH IS THAT FOOD...
EVERYONE LOST CONTROL OF THEMSELVES ...
... JUST BY LOOKING AT IT!
THIS GUY ...
IT WAS THAT APPLE!
THAT...
...IS ONE OF THE DISHES IN ACACIA'S FULL-COURSE MEAL!

WHA...
WHAAAAT?!

OH, SORRY. THAT WAS A LIE.
HUH
YOU...
YOU JERK! THERE ARE LIES YOU CAN TELL, AND THOSE YOU CAN'T!
BUT...
...IT HAS THE SMELL OF IT.
UH...
THAT IS JUST AN APPLE, BUT...
...THE TINIEST WHIFF OF A DISH FROM ACACIA'S FULL-COURSE MEAL...
...LINGERS ON IT.
THAT... THAT APPLE...
... HAS ITS SMELL ...?
THE REASON WHY THERE WAS NO DOUBT AS TO THE CREDIBILITY OF THAT STATEMENT...
...IS BECAUSE THE FIVE MEN WHO WERE UTTERLY TRANSFIXED ...
...BY THAT ABSOLUTELY ORDINARY APPLE...
...COULD FEEL IT.

ALL THIS FROM A LINGERING SCENT ON JUST ONE LITTLE APPLE!
THE REAL THING IS A LOT MORE ENTICING.
BDMP
BDMP
AND IN THE PLACE YOU'RE HEADED TO...
BDMP
BDMP
...THERE ARE LOTS OF FOODS LIKE THAT WAITING FOR YOU!
I...
I JUST...
I JUST SPENT SIX MONTHS IN THE GOURMET WORLD, BUT NOTHING SHOCKED MY SENSES LIKE THAT.
HEH HEH... IT WAS DURING THE "DAY," AND YOU ONLY WENT TO SAFE SPOTS, RIGHT?
BDMP
YOU AREN'T LYING. FOR THE SMELL TO BE SO POTENT...
...WE MUST BE TALKING ABOUT ACACIA'S FULL-COURSE MEAL. IT'S A WORLD APART FROM OTHER FOODS!
BDMP

HOW ABOUT IT?
LET'S EAT THIS TOGETHER...
...AS THE MEAL BEFORE YOUR DEPARTURE.
EVEN IF IT'S JUST A PLAIN OLD APPLE.
YES, LET'S EAT!
THEN I'LL CUT IT INTO APPLE RABBITS.
S...STOP! YOU MUSTN'T DO THAT TO SUCH A SACRED APPLE.
WHAT-EVER, IT'S JUST AN ORDINARY APPLE.
I'LL EAT IT IN ONE BITE.
NO WAY, YOU IDIOT!
S...SINCE THIS IS SUCH A RARE CHANCE...
...WHY DON'T I PREPARE SOME THINGS TO ENJOY ALONG WITH IT?
YEAH! GOOD IDEA, KOMATSU!
CHICHI! WOULD IT BE ALL RIGHT IF I USED YOUR INGREDIENTS AND KITCHEN?
HM? SURE, WHATEVER. USE IT ALL YOU LIKE.
I FIGURED YOU'D BE USING THIS PLACE...
...AT THE START OF YOUR JOURNEY ANYWAY.
HUH?
OH, AND ALSO, CHICHI.
YOU SAID YOU WERE A FLAVOR HERMIT, RIGHT?
I DON'T QUITE UNDERSTAND WHAT THAT MEANS, BUT...
...YOU'RE A CHEF, I TAKE IT? IF IT'S ALL RIGHT WITH YOU, WOULD YOU COOK WITH ME?

LISTEN, YOU... "FLAVOR HERMIT" IS A VERY IMPORTANT TITLE. DON'T MAKE LIGHT OF IT.
AND ALL LITTLE ICHI ASKED OF ME...
...WAS TO HAVE YOU EAT THIS APPLE. THAT'S ALL!
I'M NOT DOING A SINGLE THING MORE FOR YOU GUYS. IT'S TOO MUCH TROUBLE!
AWW, BUT...
THERE'S SO MUCH WE WANT TO ASK YOU, CHICHI.
LIKE WHAT EXACTLY YOU ARE, FOR STARTERS...
ALL YOUR ANSWERS ARE IN THE GOURMET WORLD.
I GAVE YOU MY CHEF'S UNIFORM! WITH NONO'S SCENT ON IT!
PERK
I'LL GO FIND EVEN MORE GIRL-SCENTED CLOTHES FOR YOU!
YOU MEAN IT?
THICK WITH THEIR SMELL?
I DO!
THEY'LL BE SATURATED!
A...AND I'LL ASK RIN FOR YOU!
MAYBE SHE'S GOT SOME PAJAMAS SHE'S DONE WITH.
ONES PACKED WITH HER SMELL!
M...ME TOO!
MY FORTUNE-TELLING BUSINESS ATTRACTS A LOT OF FEMALE CLIENTS.
I'LL ASK THEM IF THEY HAVE ANYTHING SOAKED IN THEIR SMELL FOR YOU.
...

Y...YOU GUUUYS!
YOU'RE SO GOOD TO ME!
AAAA
IT'S SO GOOD TO BE ALIVE!
ALL RIGHTY THEN! IF YOU MEAN IT, THEN I'LL COOK!
HURRAY! LET'S GET COOKING!
FOR YOUR LAST SUPPER!
"LAST"?!

JUST LIKE WHEN...
...THE FIVE OF YOU SEARCHED ...
...FOR THE ENTRANCE TO THIS ROOM...
...IF YOU DON'T POOL YOUR STRENGTHS, YOU'LL NEVER GET WHAT YOU'RE AFTER.
THE GOURMET WORLD AT "NIGHT" AS IT IS NOW...
...IS THAT KIND OF PLACE.
EVEN THE STRENGTH OF THE MONSTERS WILL DIFFER FROM DURING THE DAY.
IF YOU'RE READY, THEN GO FOR IT!
TAKE THE FIRST STEP OF YOUR JOURNEY!

HERE WE COME, GOURMET WORLD!
BRRKK
OH, IT'S AWAKE. PERFECT TIMING.
YEAH!!

TORIKO

GOURMET CHECKLIST

Vol. 295

RESERVOIR SEA CUCUMBER
(MOLLUSK)

CAPTURE LEVEL: 1

HABITAT: ECO LAND

SIZE: 35 CM

HEIGHT: ---

WEIGHT: 30 KG

PRICE: 9,000 YEN

DANGLE
I GET MY WATER FROM A RESERVOIR SEA CUCUMBER.
BY DUNKING IT IN THE RIVER FOR TEN SECONDS, IT FILTERS AND STORES UP TO THIRTY LITERS OF WATER.
BLOOP
VERY HANDY.

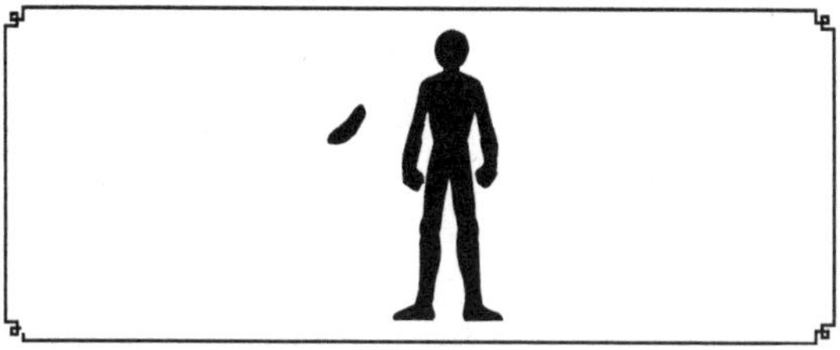

SCALE

DUNK A RESERVOIR SEA CUCUMBER IN A RIVER FOR TEN SECONDS AND IT WILL STORE AND FILTER UP TO THIRTY LITERS OF WATER. IT'S USED IN PLACE OF TAP WATER IN ECO LAND, AND IN ARID OR DROUGHT-STRICKEN REGIONS, IT CAN SERVE AS AN EMERGENCY WATER SUPPLY. THE RESERVOIR SEA CUCUMBER IS BOTH ECOLOGICAL AND CONVENIENT.

THOOM
GOURMET 272: TO WHERE DREAMS AWAIT!!
BOOM
CRMBL CRMBL
KRIK KRAK
ZOOP
?!
RMBL
RMBL
WH...
WHAT THE ?!
RRMBL
SHOOM
OH, IT'S AWAKE.
PERFECT TIMING.

KWOOM
GOURMET 272: TO WHERE DREAMS AWAIT!!
OCTOMELON*
(MOLLUSK FRUIT)
CAPTURE LEVEL 265

 *SUBMITTED BY KENTARO FROM NIIGATA!

"CAMPER MONSTER"?!
WHAT IS THAT?
THAT'S RIGHT.
IT SLEEPS UNDER-GROUND UNTIL ITS FRUIT BODY HAS RIPENED.
I'M JUST GLAD IT POPPED UP IN TIME FOR YOUR DEPARTURE.
IT WILL BE YOUR TENT ON THE FIRST LEG OF YOUR JOURNEY...
...THROUGH THE GOURMET WORLD.
T... TENT?!
THIS OCTOPUS?!
ER, OR IS IT A WATER-MELON?!
THERE'S NO WAY! IT'S TOO BIG!
DON'T UNDER-ESTIMATE THE WONDERS OF THE OCTO-MELON!
THE FOUR OF YOU ARE CAPABLE MEN.
DO YOU THINK YOUR INABILITY TO FIND THIS PLACE...
...AND THE ENTRANCE TO MY HOME...
...WAS PURE COINCIDENCE?
!
THE OCTOMELON HAS ANOTHER NAME--SAFETY MONSTER.

EVEN IN THE HARSHEST GOURMET WORLD ENVIRONMENTS...
?
...IT CAN CLOAK ITS BODY AND MAKE ITSELF INTO A SAFE ZONE...
...MAKING IT HARD FOR OTHER CREATURES TO DETECT OR ATTACK IT.
AND ALTHOUGH IT DOES GET DETECTED BY CREATURES WITH CAPTURE LEVELS HIGHER THAN ITS OWN...
...IT SHOULD SERVE AS A SUITABLE ENOUGH SLEEPING AREA FOR YOU ON YOUR WAY INTO THE GOURMET WORLD.
LITTLE ICHI...
...PREPARED IT FOR YOU.
!
...
THE OLD MAN...
WHAT A SOFTY FOR HIS PUPILS, I SWEAR.
THOUGH AFTER MEETING YOU, I CAN SEE WHY.

IT'S THANKS TO YOU...
...THAT LITTLE ICHI COULD PASS AWAY WITH NO REGRETS.
THE BATON HAS BEEN PASSED TO YOU!
IT'S YOU WHO MUST REACH THE FINISH LINE!
NOW GO!
YOUR FRIENDS ARE WAITING FOR YOU AT THE PORT!
UH... UM...
CHICHI ...
WHAT WILL YOU DO NOW?
I'M GOING TO A SOCIAL.
YOU'RE GOING OUT DRINKING?!
WITH SOME FEMALE BEETLES.
WE'LL TOAST WITH TREE SAP.
HAVE YOU NO STAN-DARDS?!

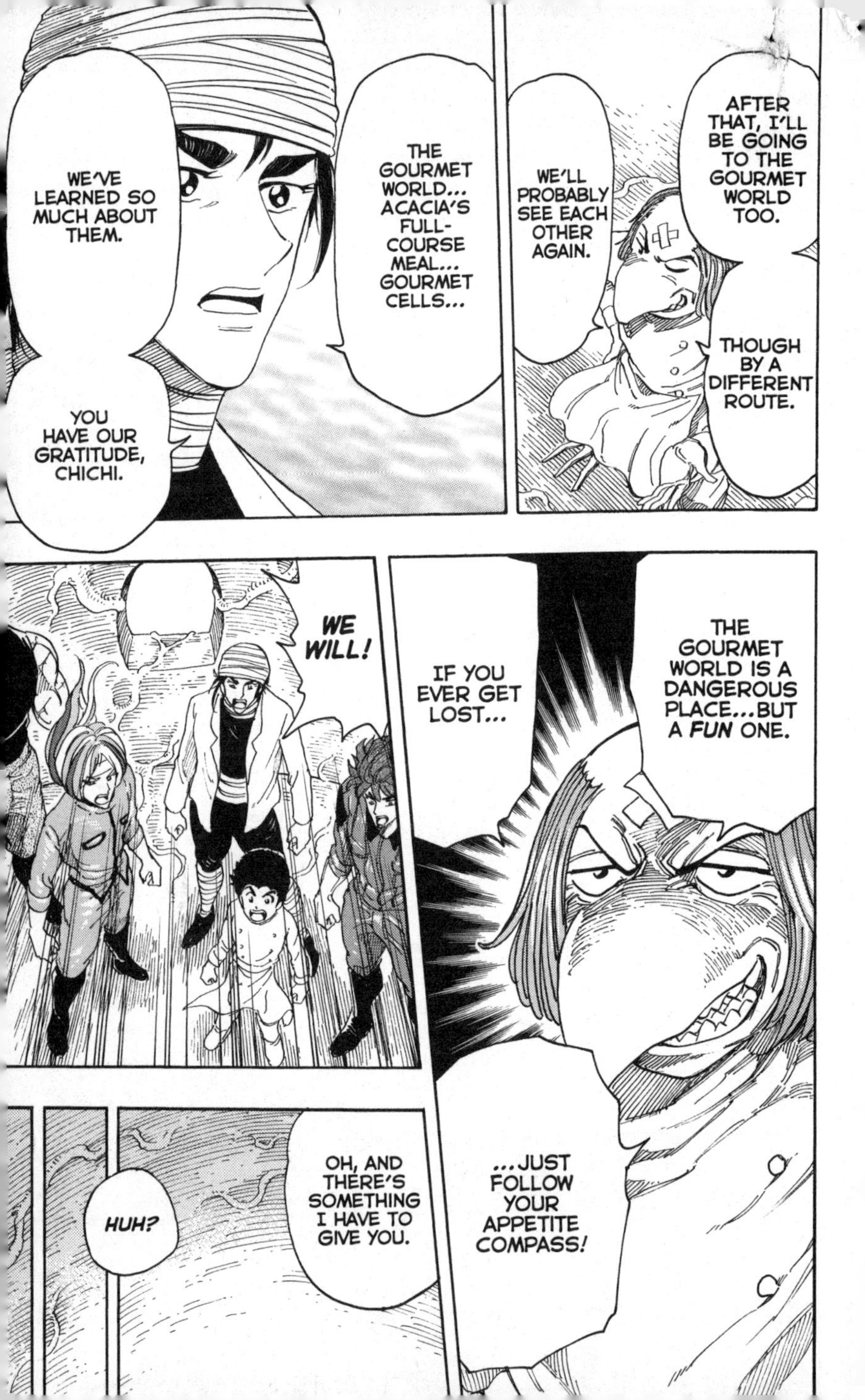
AFTER THAT, I'LL BE GOING TO THE GOURMET WORLD TOO.
THOUGH BY A DIFFERENT ROUTE.
WE'LL PROBABLY SEE EACH OTHER AGAIN.
THE GOURMET WORLD... ACACIA'S FULL-COURSE MEAL... GOURMET CELLS...
WE'VE LEARNED SO MUCH ABOUT THEM.
YOU HAVE OUR GRATITUDE, CHICHI.
THE GOURMET WORLD IS A DANGEROUS PLACE...BUT A *FUN* ONE.
IF YOU EVER GET LOST...
...JUST FOLLOW YOUR APPETITE COMPASS!
WE WILL!
OH, AND THERE'S SOMETHING I HAVE TO GIVE YOU.
HUH?

GOURMET HUNTER HARBOR

PORT TORIKO
GOURMET HUNTER TORIKO HAD DISCOVERED MORE NEW FOODS THAN ANYONE.
RKKMM
TORIKO, LOOK AT...
...THE PORT...
I KNOW... JUST LOOK.
EVERY-ONE CAME...
...TO SEE US OFF!

TORIKO HAD SET OFF ON SO MANY JOURNEYS FROM THIS PORT THAT THEY NAMED IT AFTER HIM.
IT WAS THE SAME PORT THAT SAW TORIKO AND KOMATSU OFF ON THEIR JOURNEY TO THE BARON ARCHIPELAGO.
TORIKO!

SO YOU'RE REALLY GOING...
OBVIOUSLY, BUT STILL...
SORRY, RIN.
I'M NOT TRYING TO MAKE A HEADACHE FOR YOU, BUT WHILE WE'RE AWAY...
...PLEASE TAKE CARE OF...
...THE HUMAN WORLD...
...AND THE WEDDING PREPARATIONS!
I WILL! ♡
IT'LL BE THE BEST DARN WEDDING YOU EVER SAW!
HA HA! I'LL COME BACK WITH GOD TO PUT ON OUR WEDDING CAKE!
I CAN'T WAIT! ♡
TORIKO.
I PACKED YOU A FEW ESSENTIALS, INCLUDING CAPTURE LEVEL MEASURING DEVICES.
OH, THANKS, PRESIDENT MANSOM.
THE ENVIRONMENT OF THE GOURMET WORLD IS AN ANIMAL IN ITS OWN RIGHT.
TORIKO, Y'ALL LEAVE AN AURA-LIKE "MARKING" IN YOUR WAKE.
STRONG MONSTERS AREN'T LIKELY TO GO NEAR IT.

I'M GONNA ASK YOU TO SEND FOOD FROM THE GOURMET WORLD TO THE HUMAN WORLD ALONG THAT ROUTE ON A REGULAR BASIS.
WE'LL BE READY TO RECEIVE WHAT YOU GIVE.
WHAT'S MORE, THAT ROUTE WILL MAKE IT EASIER FOR OTHER CAPABLE FOLKS TO ENTER THE GOURMET WORLD.
GOURMET WORLD
HUMAN WORLD
WE'LL BE RIGHT BEHIND YOU.
THANKS FOR LEADING THE WAY, TORIKO.
I'LL BE WAIT-ING.
AIMARU.
THE ONE WHO'S GONNA BE RIGHT BEHIND YOU...
...IS THE GREAT ZONGEH!
I MIGHT EVEN OVER-TAKE YOU!
YOU TAKE CARE TOO, KOMA-TSU.
I WILL, TAKI-MARU.
NOBODY'S LISTENING, MASTER ZONGEH.
...

CHEF KOMATSU, HERE... IT'S A ***WHETSTONE APRON*** AND ***WHETSTONE BOOTS*** SO YOU CAN SHARPEN YOUR BLADES WHENEVER YOU WANT.
THEY'RE GOOD FOR AN ALMOST INDEFINITE NUMBER OF SHARPENINGS. PLEASE TAKE THEM WITH YOU.
MELK! THANK YOU SO MUCH!
I SWEAR MY MELK BLADE...
...WILL PREPARE ACACIA'S FULL-COURSE MEAL!
I CAN'T WAIT!
HARMONY'S IMPORTANT, EVEN IN THE GOURMET WORLD.
ARE YOUR RECORD COPIES IN ORDER, SUNNY?
YEP. THANKS, PONKOCHI.
I COPIED THEM ALL.
MR. ZEBRA...
PLEASE BE CAREFUL...
SAND GARDEN VILLAGERS
HUH? WHO ARE YOU GUYS?
WE'LL HAVE YOUR BACK SOON.
AFTER WE EAT ENOUGH DELICIOUS FOOD TO BE ABLE TO FOLLOW YOU.
MATCH.
DON'T WORRY, WE'LL SEND TONS OF FOOD BACK.

IF YOU'RE WORRIED ABOUT HOW THE HUMAN WORLD WILL PREPARE GOURMET WORLD INGREDIENTS...
...REST ASSURED THEY'RE IN GOOD HANDS!
ZSH
!
LEAVE IT TO US CHEFS OF THE HUMAN WORLD!
GUYS!
YUUUUN!
YUN YUN
WADDL WADDL
YUN! COME WITH ME!
ALL RIGHT, LET'S GO!
TERRY!!
LET'S GO!
KISS!!
WE'RE GOING NOW!
QUINN!!

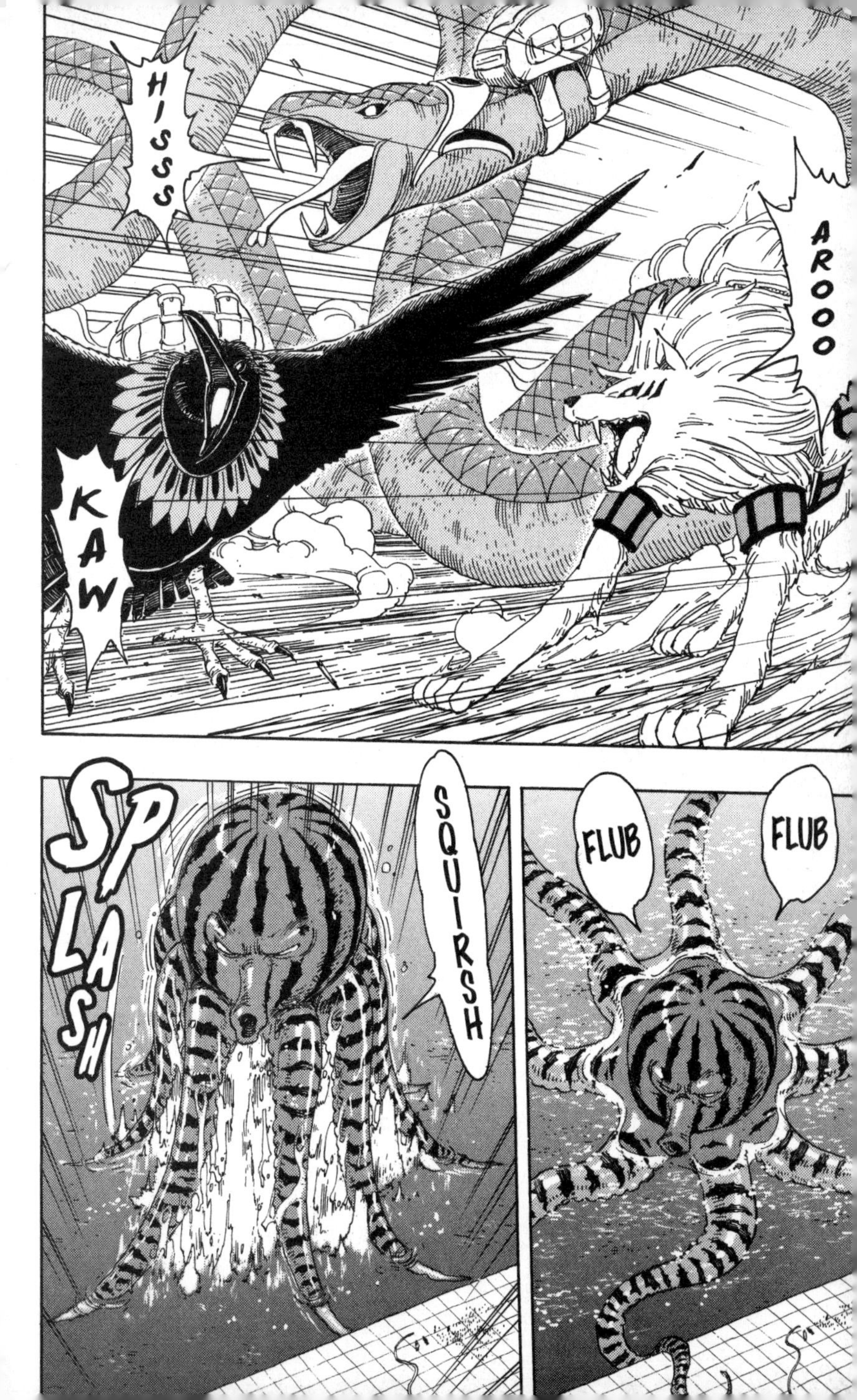
AROOO
HISSS
KAW
FLUB
FLUB
SQUIRSH
SPLASH

ALL ABOARD!
TERRY AND THE OTHERS GET THE OCTO-MELON'S BELLY ROOM!!
HOP
OKAY, EVERY-BODY!
WE'RE OFF!
WE'RE HEADED TO A PLACE...
WE'RE LEAVING FROM THIS PLACE...
...FILLED WITH OUR MEMORIES ...
...WHERE EVERYONE'S DREAMS AWAIT!

TO THE GOURMET WORLD!!

SHUO
OFF WE GOOO!!
I...
I'M...

...GOING TO CAPTURE ACACIA'S MAIN DISH, GOD!
AND COMPLETE MY LIFE'S FULL-COURSE MEAL!
I WILL CAPTURE ACACIA'S DRINK...
ATOM !!
I'LL CAPTURE ACACIA'S DESSERT ...
EARTH !!
HMPH. I'LL EAT ANYTHING IF IT'S GOOD.
AND PUT IT IN MY FULL-COURSE MEAL!
YOU BETTER ADAPT TO ME, GOURMET WORLD!!

I'M GOING TO TAKE ALL OF THAT...
...AND PREPARE IT!!
FIRST STOP, THE THIRD ENTRANCE TO THE GOURMET WORLD!!
YUTO ISLAND'S BAY OF EVIL SPIRITS!
LET'S GO!!
TO BE CONTINUED!

TORIKO

GOURMET CHECKLIST

Vol. 296

FIRE MOSS BALLS
(ALGAE)

CAPTURE LEVEL: 2
HABITAT: ECO LAND
SIZE: 5 CM
HEIGHT: ---
WEIGHT: 10 G
PRICE: 5,000 YEN

WHEN I WANT A SIMPLE FIRE, I USE THESE FIRE MOSS BALLS.
IF YOU RUB THEM AGAINST EACH OTHER, THEY IGNITE AND CAN KEEP BURNING FOR FORTY MINUTES.
FOOM
PLUS YOU WASH, DRY AND REUSE THEM.

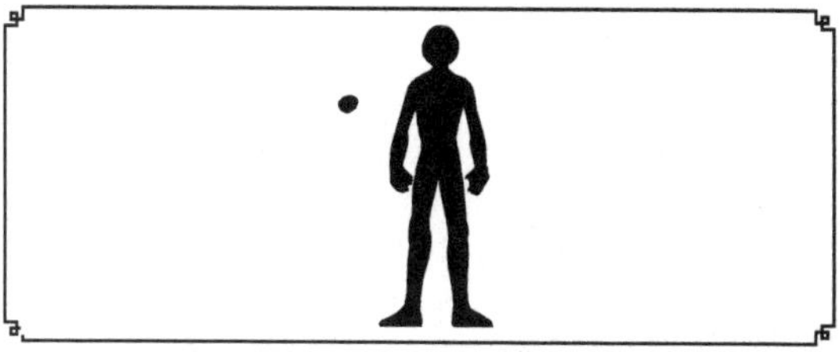

SCALE

WHEN YOU RUB FIRE MOSS BALLS AGAINST EACH OTHER, THEY IGNITE AND CAN CONTINUE BURNING FOR UP TO FORTY MINUTES. THEY'RE ESSENTIAL FOR COOKING IN ECO LAND. AFTER BEING WASHED AND DRIED, THEY CAN BE REUSED. UNLIKE TYPICAL GAS STOVES, FIRE MOSS BALLS COOK MORE LIKE A HIGH-GRADE CHARCOAL THAT USES FAR INFRARED EFFECT TO DELICIOUSLY GRILL FOOD. HENCE WHY MANY CHEFS OUTSIDE OF ECO LAND USE FIRE MOSS BALLS FOR THEIR COOKING TOO.

COMING NEXT VOLUME

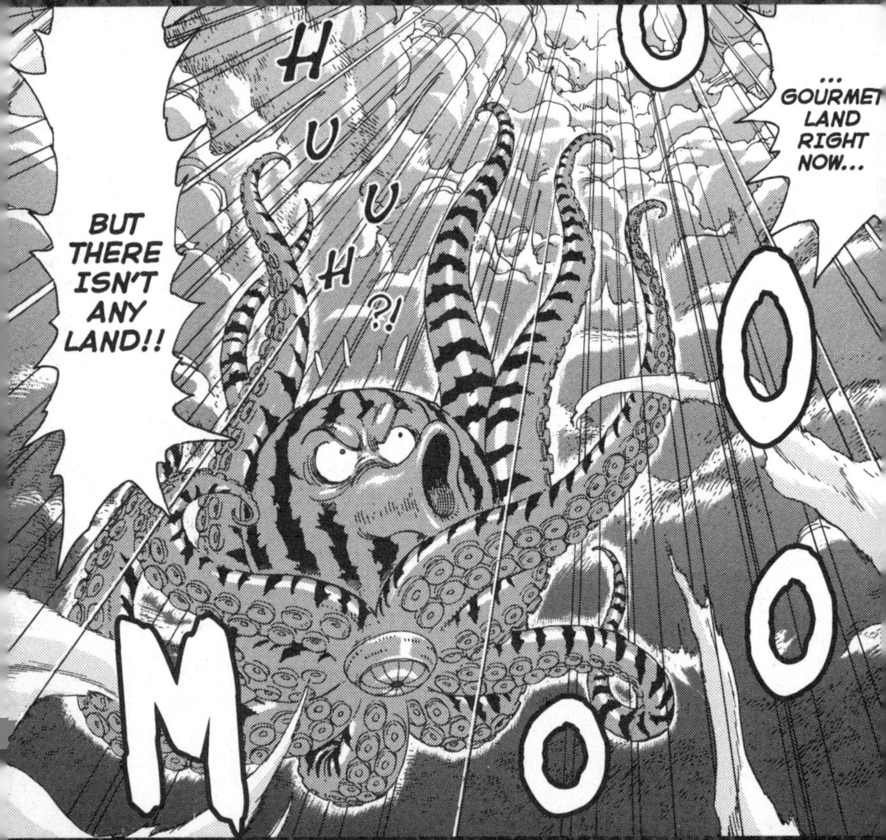

HEX FOOD WORLD

To feed the starving Human World, Toriko, his chef partner Komatsu and the other Four Kings journey to the Gourmet World. But getting to the Gourmet World proves quite the challenge! Even on the back of their trusty Octomelon, they may not survive the barbed waves of the Thorned Sea or its ghostly floating ships—much less the tricks of the giant floating faces on the land itself. And did we mention there isn't any land?

AVAILABLE DECEMBER 2015!

The latest manga from the creator of Dragon Ball
JACO
THE GALACTIC PATROLMAN
Includes a special chapter revealing the secret of Goku's origins!
STORY AND ART BY
Akira Toriyama
Retired scientist Omori lives alone on a deserted island while continuing his research into time-travel. His quiet life is interrupted when galactic patrolman Jaco crash-lands and decides to move in with him. This agent from space claims to be elite, but sometimes it can be a little hard to believe. Can Jaco get along with the old man long enough to save the earth from a dangerous threat?
JACO THE GALACTIC PATROLMAN
SHONEN JUMP MANGA
Akira Toriyama
VIZ media
SHONEN JUMP
RATED ALL AGES
www.viz.com
www.shonenjump.com
ratings.viz.com
JACO THE GALACTIC PATROLMAN © 2013 by BIRD STUDIO/SHUEISHA Inc.

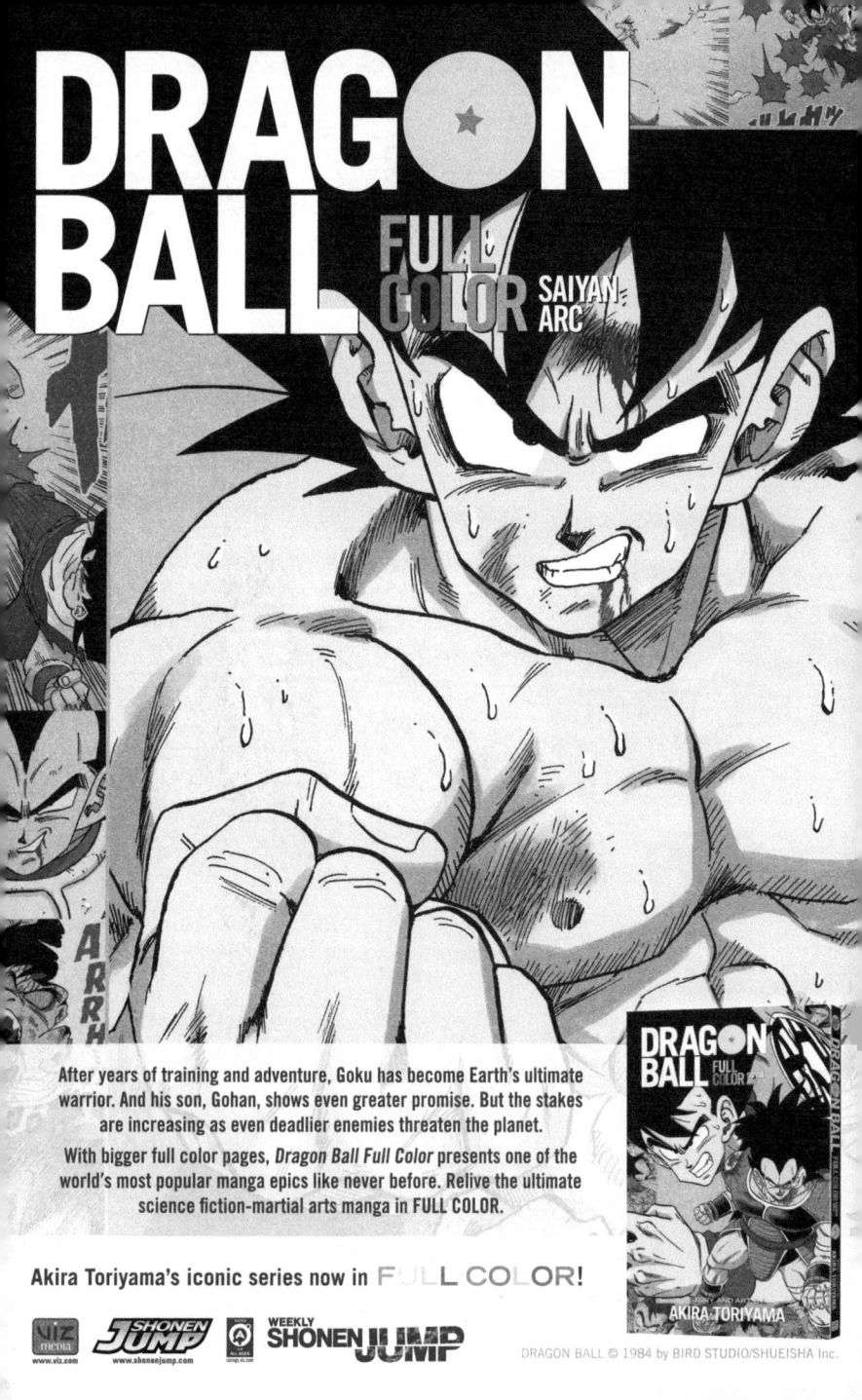

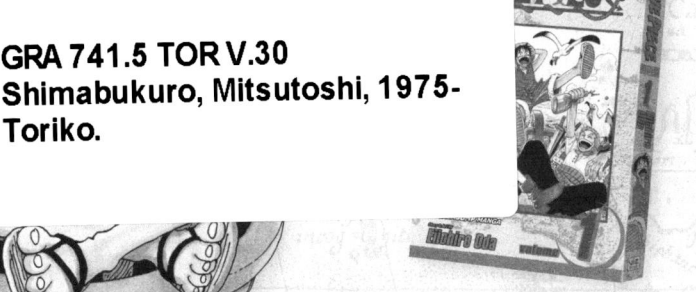

You're Reading in the Wrong Direction!!

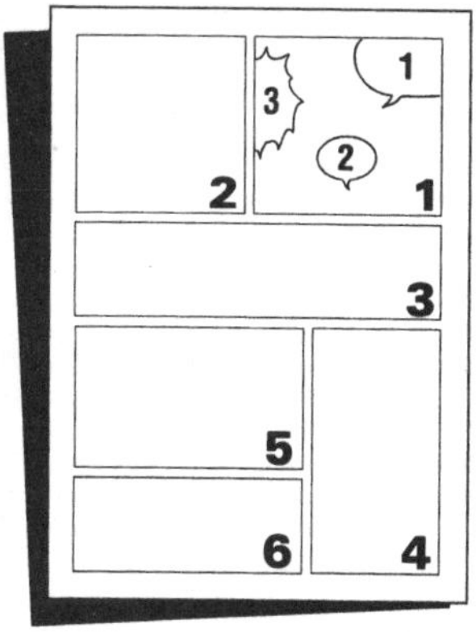

Whoops! Guess what? You're starting at the wrong end of the comic!

...It's true! In keeping with the original Japanese format, **Toriko** is meant to be read from right to left, starting in the upper-right corner.

Unlike English, which is read from left to right, Japanese is read from right to left, meaning that action, sound effects and word-balloon order are completely reversed... something which can make readers unfamiliar with Japanese feel pretty backwards themselves. For this reason, manga or Japanese comics published in the U.S. in English have sometimes been published "flopped"—that is, printed in exact reverse order, as though seen from the other side of a mirror.

By flopping pages, U.S. publishers can avoid confusing readers, but the compromise is not without its downside. For one thing, a character in a flopped manga series who once wore in the original Japanese version a T-shirt emblazoned with "M A Y" (as in "the merry month of") now wears one which reads "Y A M"! Additionally, many manga creators in Japan are themselves unhappy with the process, as some feel the mirror-imaging of their art skews their original intentions.

We are proud to bring you Mitsutoshi Shimabukuro's **Toriko** in the original unflopped format. For now, though, turn to the other side of the book and let the adventure begin...!

—Editor

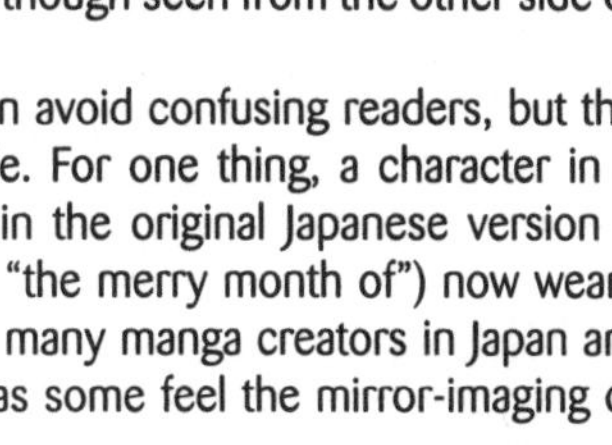